{ **75** Recipes Made Without Eggs, Gluten, Soy, or Refined Sugar }

dairy·free

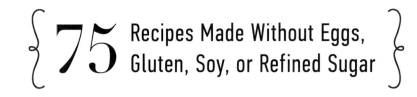

Ice Cream

written & photographed by

KELLY V. BROZYNA

author of TheSpunkyCoconut.com

VICTORY BELT PUBLISHING INC.

Las Vegas

First Published in 2014 by Victory Belt Publishing Inc.

ISBN-13: 978-1-628600-39-1

This book is for entertainment purposes. The publisher and author of this cookbook are not responsible in any manner whatsoever for any adverse effects arising directly or indirectly as a result of the information provided in this book.

Printed in the U.S.A.

RRD 0114

To my readers,

with loving appreciation.

♥

Contents

Preface

Hi! I'm Kelly, and I'm so excited to share my dairy-free ice cream book with you! As you may know from my other cookbooks and my website, TheSpunkyCoconut.com, I'm crazy about ice cream. I've been experimenting with dairy-free ice cream since about 2005, when my family and I stopped eating dairy (as well as gluten and refined sugar) in attempt to regain our health. I had been diagnosed with celiac disease, and my husband had ADHD. Our youngest daughter had been diagnosed with autism and global delay, and our oldest daughter with failure to thrive and behavioral problems. We have overcome all our health problems with great success through diet and biomedical treatments.

I always say that it was harder for me to give up dairy than it was to give up gluten. Giving up gluten is easy once you break the sugar/carb addiction that comes with eating grains, but I really missed dairy.

In 2007 I got into raw food with my health mentor, Cheryl, and her assistant, Reilley. Raw foodists use coconut, nuts, seeds, and dates to create all sorts of dairy-free recipes. I'll never forget the first time Reilley brought me a raw cheesecake that she had made with soaked cashews and coconut oil. It blew my mind. But I didn't want to stay completely raw forever. I craved cooked food again. I'm a firm believer in eating intuitively.

So I took the concepts that I admired from raw food recipes and brought them into my less restrictive kitchen. I made cream sauce, cheese, yogurt, and ice cream—all without dairy. As time went by, we became more and more turned off by the idea of consuming cow milk. Other animals don't breastfeed for life, nor do they consume the breast milk of another species. It makes sense that milk from another species is hard to digest, mucus-forming, and especially problematic for celiacs since the protein (casein) is almost identical to gluten on a molecular level.

Through research and practice, I learned so much about making dairy-free ice cream. My objective was to make the creamiest, most divine ice cream while keeping it healthy and allergen-free. When my gluten- and dairy-eating extended family members say that this is the best ice cream of any kind that they've ever had, I know that it's good enough to share with you.

Happy dairy-free ice cream eating!

♥, Kelly

A history of dairy-free ice cream

When Kelly told me that she planned to write an ice cream book, I became immediately interested in learning the history of frozen desserts. Much has been written on the charming history of ice cream, but the story of dairy-free ice cream is more obscure. I have written this brief essay to share its unique history with our casein-free, lactose-intolerant, Paleo, and vegan readers—or anyone who is interested in food history.

Various ancient cultures are known to have enjoyed flavored drinks mixed with ice shavings or snow. It was the development of a sixteenth-century technique to artificially freeze food—using a mixture of crushed ice and salt to create a freezing effect—that allowed true ice creams and dessert ices to be prepared in the kitchen. In the 1600s, specialized containers, tools, and training spread across Europe. Dairy-free ices and sorbets were all the rage among the European aristocracy during the seventeenth and eighteenth centuries. The flavored ices were typically formed in elaborate molds and set as table centerpieces to delight dinner guests. French and Italian chefs became particularly known for their ices.

At the same time, chefs were using their custard recipes to create milk-based ice creams. Interestingly, the very first ice cream cookbook discussed nut ingredients. In 1768 a Monsieur Emy published an untitled book in which he describes how to infuse the flavors of almonds and cashews into ice cream. This early chef praised the taste and health benefits of nuts, and almond milk had been a common beverage in Europe since the fifteenth century. Yet before the twentieth century, there seems to have been no interest in developing nondairy nut-based ice creams.

While ices have been prepared at home and sold commercially for as long as ice cream, it was the frozen dairy treats that went on to dominate the kitchen and the market.

At the end of the nineteenth century, Ellen G. White preached against the large quantities of milk and sugar that Americans ate. In the twentieth century, members of her Seventh-day Adventist Church published some pioneering cookbooks advocating nondairy ice cream recipes. In 1936, Adventist Dr. John Harvey Kellogg printed a soymilk ice cream recipe in his *Good Health* magazine. In the same year, Dorothea Van Gundy self-published an Adventist cookbook, *La Sierra Recipes,* to promote her family's soy business. The book included vanilla, avocado-orange, and almond-soy ice cream flavors.

Jethro Kloss included a single soymilk ice cream recipe in his 1939 best-selling cookbook *Back to Eden.* Kloss focused on soy as the preferred substitute for dairy, but his book mentioned that a milk could also be made from almonds. Dorothea Van Gundy published another book in 1963 called *The Soybean Cookbook* that featured five soy ice creams.

In 1968, *The Ten Talents* was perhaps the first published cookbook to include nut-based ice creams. Authors Frank and Rosalie Hurd developed ice cream recipes that relied on almonds, cashews, and coconut.

Hundreds of thousands of copies of *The Soybean Cookbook* were sold. *Back to Eden* and

The Ten Talents sold equally well, and they are still in print today.

Seventh-day Adventists have avoided milk to support good health—an important point in their theology. The Jewish community has served dairy-free iced treats as part of its own religious observance. Kosher laws forbid the consumption of dairy and meat in the same meal. Eating a dairy ice cream even a few hours after a hamburger could be a no-no, so ices have long filled the role of frozen dessert. Several companies in 1920s New York City sold kosher dairy ice cream (to be eaten away from meats). They quickly started offering dairy-free ices as well. Eggs were used to create a creamy texture, but they were replaced by soy lecithin in the early 1940s. In the later 1940s, Jewish caterers, ice cream shops, and housewives were using Rich's Whip Topping, the first commercially available soy-based whipped topping, to create nondairy ice creams.

Early interest in soy wasn't limited to religious groups. The aforementioned Rich's Whip Topping was developed using soymilk research conducted by Henry Ford. It may be surprising to learn that the founder of the Ford Motor Company had a personal interest in soybeans. In the early 1930s, he built a soymilk plant and recruited scientists to study soybeans' commercial potential. They developed a way to make plastic automobile parts from soy, but they also looked into food. At the 1934 Chicago World's Fair, Ford's exhibit served experimental tofu ice cream. World War II forced Ford's program to abandon its soy food research, but its discoveries influenced future soy ice cream makers.

In 1945, health-food advocate Mildred Lager published *The Useful Soybean,* which offered a soymilk and coconut milk ice cream recipe. Lager's unpublished soymilk ice cream recipes were later adapted by Dorothea Van Gundy for her *Soybean Cookbook.*

Many state legislatures had enacted regulations that made it difficult for dairy-free ventures to get started. For instance, dairy-free ice creams weren't officially allowed to be sold in New York until 1968 because of the technicality that there was no existing legal standard to follow. And until 1976, California's department of agriculture would not allow nondairy ice cream to be sold in soft-serve machines. Careful petitioning by nondairy ice cream producers across the country quickly opened up the legality for their new dairy-free products. It is interesting to note that the word *ice cream* is not allowed on today's packaging of commercially sold dairy-free desserts. State departments of agriculture require the less romantic term *nondairy frozen dessert.*

In the last quarter of the twentieth century, popular interest in the vegetarian diet, the vegan diet, and overall healthy eating grew. Dairy-free ice cream became more common, but the recipes continued to depend on soy. While soymilk creates a great texture for ice cream, it comes with a variety of problems. Soy is difficult to digest, is mucus-forming, and contains phytoestrogens, which influence a person's hormonal balance. What's more, soy plants grown in the United States are most often genetically modified organisms, and many people suffer from an allergy to soy.

Around the turn of the century, raw foodists began promoting dairy-free recipes that are consciously soy-free. *Raw: The Uncookbook* (1999) by Juliano Brotman includes three frozen treats—gelato, ice cream, and a torte. All are based on blended nuts, nut butter, coconut, or fruit. Many raw books by other authors appeared in the 2000s, and they often included similarly prepared ice cream recipes.

In the twenty-first century, popular interest in dairy-free ice cream is at its peak. The trailblazing Adventist food community and the early-adopting kosher community have been

No. 589. Chrysanthemum.

No. 365. Daisy Bunch.

No. 310. Sea Shell.

Hinged pewter molds for ices and ice cream were popular in the 1800s.

joined by vegans, raw foodists, Paleo dieters, the casein intolerant, the lactose intolerant, and the generally health conscious. Today's health food stores commonly carry ice creams made from coconut milk, hemp milk, rice milk, and soymilk. In recent years, a flurry of devoted nondairy frozen dessert shops have opened, delighting the dairy-free crowd in cities across the United States and Europe.

Kelly's *Dairy-Free Ice Cream* takes the best from each of these historic dairy-free ice cream traditions. The recipes in this book feature an ice cream base of coconut and nuts, but Kelly's particular method doesn't require the time and expense of strict raw food preparation. Her ice creams avoid the problematic soy found in Adventist and vegan cookbooks but take advantage of their concept of using a nondairy milk for a smooth texture. In addition to original flavors, Kelly provides old favorites that you would expect to find in a conventional-dairy ice cream cookbook. She accomplishes the right sweetness without the customarily enormous amounts of unhealthy white sugar. I'm sure you will enjoy Kelly's innovative contribution to the library of dairy-free ice cream cookbooks.

Cheers,
Andrew Brozyna

FURTHER READING

Aoyagi, Akiko, and Shurtleff, William. *Tofutti & Other Soy Ice Creams: The Non-Dairy Frozen Dessert Industry and Trade.* Lafayette, CA: The Soyfoods Center, 1989.

Day, Ivan. *Ice Cream.* Oxford: Shire Publications, 2011.

Quinzio, Jeri. *Of Sugar and Snow: A History of Ice Cream Making.* Berkeley: University of California Press, 2009.

A quick introduction to dairy-free ice cream

When it comes to making awesome dairy-free ice cream, there are two really important ingredients to understand: sugar and fat. Let's begin with sugar.

SUGAR

Sugar, or lack of sugar, greatly affects how hard your ice cream will freeze when stored in the freezer. Smaller amounts of sugar (whether from dates, honey, agave, or fruit) result in ice cream that freezes much harder, takes longer to defrost, and feels icier in your mouth. I have designed the ice cream recipes in this book to be as healthful as possible, and therefore to have the least amount of sugar possible, without compromising on taste or texture. If you need to reduce the sugar in the recipes for health reasons, however, I have included instructions for doing so in the Sweeteners section on page 16.

In lightly sweetened ice cream recipes like mine, the addition of a thickener can help create a smoother texture. The freezer creates ice crystals that can make your ice cream, well . . . icy. The recipes in this book that use dates but don't contain additional sugar sources like bananas, 100-percent juice, or figs benefit from thickener, which helps prevent ice crystals from forming. These ice crystals are not as much of a problem when the ice cream is eaten immediately after being made, straight from the ice cream machine. I explain which thickeners I use and how to use them in the Thickeners section on page 19.

Most of the ice cream in this book will be soft enough to scoop about twenty minutes after you take it out of the freezer (assuming that you freeze it in a shallow container, like a 6-cup rectangular glass dish). However, two of the recipes have a high enough sugar content that you can scoop them the moment you take them out of the freezer: Pomegranate Sorbet and Grape Sorbet. The Fried Banana, Fig, Rocky Road, and Mulled Cider ice creams will likely be ready to scoop in ten minutes because of their additional natural sugar content. Ice cream sandwiches need about fifteen minutes to soften before eating, and larger ice cream cakes need about an hour to soften before slicing.

Sugar also affects, to a smaller degree, how the ice cream feels in your mouth. Even more crucial to the mouthfeel, though, is fat. So let's talk about that now.

FAT

The reason why fat is important in ice cream has to do with the way it feels. Higher amounts of fat in your ice cream make it richer and creamier. Fat also triggers a positive feeling in the brain. (Really, it's true.)

The best nondairy substitute for heavy cream and/or egg yolks is full-fat coconut milk. Not only does coconut milk do an excellent job of creating that creamy mouthfeel we all want in ice cream, but it also has wonderful, healthy attributes: the fat in coconut milk consists of medium-chain triglycerides, which are easily digested and converted to energy rather than stored as fat in the body; and it increases your metabolism while protecting against viruses and bacteria. These are just a few of the reasons why I love coconut.

People often ask me to be brand-specific when it comes to coconut milk. With such a huge selection of packaging and a growing number of coconut milk brands becoming available these days, the choice can be overwhelming. In the Ice Cream Base section on page 14, I list the brands I prefer and why I prefer them.

TECHNIQUE

I always recommend chilling the ice cream puree before adding it to the ice cream machine. This is especially important for purees that are warm, like Fried Banana Ice Cream, but should be done no matter what. You may find out the hard way that if you use gelatin (which is dairy-free but *not* vegetarian) as a thickener and leave the ice cream base in the refrigerator for too long, it will become like Jell-O. Don't worry; just let the puree sit on the counter until it has softened some, and then you can add it to the ice cream machine.

It's very important to store ice cream in a shallow dish in the freezer. This allows the ice cream to defrost evenly when it's time to serve. I like to use pretty casserole dishes (which are shallow) when I make ice cream for company, as seen on page 163. You can find all the equipment you need in the Tools section on page 21.

TOPPINGS

The contrast of texture, and sometimes temperature (think warm sauce), that toppings provide takes a dish of ice cream from good to great. Rather than store-bought sauces, which are often made with a long list of unrecognizable ingredients, and refined-sugar sprinkles, I make homemade sauces and sprinkled toppings. Or sometimes I simply opt for ground freeze-dried strawberries and fresh fruit, which look so pretty (see pages 198 and 202, respectively).

YIELD

I designed all the ice cream and frozen dessert recipes in this book to make 1 to 1½ quarts, because that is the most common ice cream machine size.

Key ingredients

As with preparing any other type of food, using good-quality, organic ingredients creates the best-tasting and best-for-you nondairy frozen treats. I always buy organic ingredients and use only natural food coloring. You can find all my favorite brands in the Resources section on page 208.

Ice cream base

In these ice cream recipes, I prefer to combine coconut milk with almond, cashew, or hemp milk to prevent the coconut flavor from overpowering the recipes. Unlike other dairy-free ice cream books, I don't use soy. Soy is hard to digest, mucus-forming, high in phytoestrogens, and one of the top food allergens.

COCONUT MILK (and Cream)

My ice creams are based primarily on full-fat coconut milk (or coconut cream that I've extracted from the milk). I use Natural Value coconut milk (found in cans) and Aroy-D Coconut Cream (actually a thick 100-percent coconut milk found in cartons) because they are BPA-free and will separate every time so that I can make whipped coconut cream. Higher-fat coconut milks like these make much richer, creamier ice cream. Avoid other kinds of coconut milk in cartons, as they are too watery.

ALMOND, CASHEW, & HEMP MILK

I combine coconut milk with almond, cashew, or hemp milk so that the coconut flavor doesn't overpower the ice cream. Almond, cashew, and hemp milk can be made at home; almond and hemp milks can also be store-bought. It's difficult to taste the almond or cashew milk when used as directed in my ice cream recipes, but hemp milk does add a slight flavor of its own, which I really like. The main reason for using hemp milk (as opposed to almond or cashew), though, is to make the ice cream nut-free for people who don't tolerate nuts.

Almond milk

To make your own almond milk, soak 1 cup of raw almonds overnight in enough water to cover, plus 2 inches. In the morning, strain and rinse the almonds and discard the soaking water, which contains enzyme inhibitors. Puree the nuts with about 4 cups of purified water. Pour the liquid into a nut milk bag or cheesecloth-lined colander set over a pitcher. Lift the bag or cloth and strain the pulp. Refrigerate the milk in the pitcher. It will keep for up to four or five days. You can use the pulp to make Chocolate Heart Cookies, which you can find on TheSpunkyCoconut.com.

Cashew milk

The recipe for cashew milk is exactly the same as for almond milk, but unlike almonds, cashews don't need to be strained. Over the years I've found that cashew milk lasts longer than homemade almond milk. Both are stored in the refrigerator, but cashew milk can last for more than five days.

Hemp milk

Hemp milk can be made the same way as almond milk, but I much prefer the taste of store-bought hemp milk. As with store-bought almond milk, always buy unsweetened hemp milk. Living Harvest Tempt is my favorite brand.

Sweeteners

You can find all these sweeteners at health food stores, iHerb.com, and Amazon.com.

HOW SWEET IS THIS ICE CREAM?

Assuming six servings per recipe, or about $2/3$ cup of ice cream per person, each serving of ice cream in this book contains about 1 to 2 tablespoons of (natural) sugar. If you want to reduce the total sugar in a recipe further, cut the sweetening ingredient in half and add extra milk and stevia. For example, if a recipe calls for ½ cup dates, you can substitute ¼ cup dates, ¼ cup coconut milk, and liquid stevia (a few drops at a time) to your taste. Just remember that the less sugar the ice cream has, the icier it will be.

DATES

Dates are my preferred sweetener because they also help thicken the ice cream and make it creamier. Dates are usually sold in the produce section of the grocery store. You can substitute equal amounts of raw honey or raw agave if you prefer.

COCONUT SUGAR

I occasionally use coconut sugar when I want to add a caramel-like flavor to ice cream. Otherwise I use coconut sugar only in baking. Coconut sugar is an unrefined, low-glycemic sugar that comes from the sap of the flowering branch of a coconut tree. Once the branch is tapped, the sap flows for twenty years, making it extremely sustainable. You can substitute an equal amount of any other granulated sugar if you like.

STEVIA

Stevia is an herb that is hundreds of times sweeter than common cane sugar. Yet unlike sugar, it doesn't affect your blood sugar levels (it's a zero on the glycemic index). The stevia plant is originally from Paraguay, where people have sweetened herbal tea with its leaves for a hundred years or more. In Japan, stevia extract has been used as a sweetener in food and beverages since 1970. About a decade later, it was introduced in Europe and America.

Most of us Americans didn't grow up with stevia, so there is some suspicion of this "new" sweetener. However, more than a century of known human consumption and decades of scientific testing have established stevia's safety. You may have heard that stevia has a strong flavor, but you'll never notice it in my recipes. Liquid stevia is just like vanilla extract: they both taste terrible straight out of the bottle, but they're fantastic additions to a recipe. Combining very small amounts of liquid stevia with coconut sugar (or other natural sweeteners) allows me to keep the total sugar to a fraction of the amount found in typical ice cream recipes.

I prefer NOW Foods, NuNaturals, and SweetLeaf brands of stevia because their extracts are naturally produced using only cold purified water and filtering systems.

Thickeners

The freezer creates ice crystals that can make your ice cream icy. Guar gum and gelatin help prevent this from happening.

GUAR GUM

When a recipe lists "thickener" as an optional ingredient, guar gum is one option. Add ½ teaspoon guar gum to the blender with the other ingredients and purée. Each batch of ice cream contains about six servings, which is less than ⅛ teaspoon of guar gum per serving. I prefer guar gum to xanthan gum for two reasons: First, I prefer that guar gum comes from guar or "cluster beans," while xanthan gum comes from bacteria. And second, I prefer to use guar gum because xanthan gum bothers a lot of people, partly due to the fact that it's usually grown on corn.

UNFLAVORED GELATIN

The second option for thickener is gelatin. It's dairy-free but *not vegetarian.* Gelatin was the first thickener I used in my ice creams, and it's still the one I prefer because of its gut-healing properties. Gelatin has truly changed my daughter's life. You can read more about that under the category "Recovering Ashley" on my site, TheSpunkyCoconut.com.

For ice cream I use the (red/orange label) Great Lakes brand of gelatin, which comes from grass-fed cows. Slowly stir 1 tablespoon gelatin into ¼ cup boiling water until it's completely dissolved. Pour the mixture into the blender last, just before you purée the ice cream mixture.

 If a recipe does *not* list "optional: thickener" in the ingredients, then a thickener is not needed.

Buttery spread

If you're vegan, there are two dairy-free buttery spreads listed in the Resources section (page 208) that will work for you.

I prefer to use a clarified butter such as ghee because it has a buttery flavor but is free of casein, lactose, and unhealthy oils like canola oil. Dairy is problematic for people with celiac disease (like me) since the casein protein in milk is almost identical to gluten on a molecular level. Most people who don't tolerate casein or lactose do well with ghee.

Chocolate and cocoa powder

I use ethically sourced, organic, dairy-free chocolate bars with an 80-percent cacao content; see the Resources section (page 208). You might find it surprising to learn that the typical chocolate bar found in your local grocery store contains as little as 15-percent cacao, which is the minimum required by the U.S. Food and Drug Administration to label a candy as "chocolate." Dark, semisweet, or bittersweet chocolate needs to contain only 35-percent cacao. That stuff is really just candy, made mostly of milk, sugar, and vegetable oil.

What little cacao is found in conventional chocolate bars has been treated heavily with pesticides, and it may have been produced by slave labor. In West Africa, the largest cacao-producing region in the world, thousands of children are enslaved on cacao farms. Cacao trees and cacao beans receive more chemical pesticides than any crop other than cotton. Fair Trade organic chocolate is delicious, and eating it supports ethical and safe cacao farming. For more info on chocolate, see *The Paleo Chocolate Lovers' Cookbook*.

There are several types of cocoa powder on the market, all of which are variations of the same product. To produce cocoa powder, chocolate manufacturers place roasted, ground cacao beans in a pneumatic press that removes the cacao butter. What's left is a dry cake that contains no more than 20-percent cacao butter. This cake is crushed to make natural cocoa powder. The process for making Dutch cocoa powder includes an additional early step of soaking the cacao beans in potassium to reduce their acidity. Black cocoa powder is a Dutch-process cocoa powder that has only 10- to 12-percent cacao butter and an impressive dark color. Raw cacao powder is a natural cocoa powder that omits the roasting stage. For cakes and cookies, my main preference is for cocoa powder that is organic and Fair Trade.

Tools

BLENDER

For the best results, I highly recommend a professional blender, like a Blendtec. I've been using my Blendtec more than once a day since 2007. (Back then I think it was called a K-Tec Champ.) Compared with other similarly priced blenders, the Blendtec has the most power and is the easiest to clean. It's also shorter, allowing you to keep it on the counter under the upper cabinets. You can find the Blendtec I use under "Tools" on my site, TheSpunkyCoconut.com. That said, any blender will work for this book.

ICE CREAM MACHINE

You do need an ice cream machine to make most of the recipes in this book. I created the recipes using a 1-quart, or 2-pint, ice cream machine, which is the most common size of affordably priced ice cream machines for the home kitchen. My ice cream machine is a Cuisinart. I have a link to it under "Tools" on my site as well. I used to have the older model of the same machine and it was really loud, so I ran it in the basement. The new one seems to work exactly the same but comes in a bunch of colors. Whichever machine you choose, be sure to read the manufacturer's instructions first. The bowl must be in the freezer for twenty-four hours or more before it is ready to make ice cream.

FOOD PROCESSOR

There are six recipes in this book that require a food processor: Pistachio Ice Cream, Saffron and Rose Ice Cream, "Peanut Butter" Chocolate Ice Cream Cake, Rainbow Pops, Chocolate Hazelnut Spread, and Coconut Cream from fresh young coconuts.

SIX-CUP RECTANGULAR GLASS DISH WITH A LID

I like to use a 6-cup rectangular glass storage dish with a plastic lid to store my ice cream in the freezer. Plastic containers transfer toxins to your food and drinks, plus they break, hold odors, and are a bad choice for the environment. The shallow design of a 6-cup rectangular glass dish helps the ice cream freeze faster and defrost more evenly than a deep dish (like a loaf pan). I get mine at my local Ace Hardware store, but you can also find them online.

SPOONULA

One of the most important pieces of equipment is also one of the least expensive—a flexible silicone spatula, or "spoonula." This is the tool you use to get your ice cream out of the ice cream machine's freezer bowl without scratching and damaging its inner surface.

ICE CREAM SCOOP WITH A LEVER

Of course you can get your ice cream out of the storage dish with a big spoon rather than an ice cream scoop with a lever, but I mention this useful tool in case you're wondering how to get a pretty scoop. It makes getting a nice scoop so much easier. I use my ice cream scoop for other recipes, too, like scooping muffin batter into paper cups.

ICE POP MOLDS

I like to make ice cream and fruit pops year-round (like Almond and Chocolate Protein Pudding Pops for breakfast—see page 144). The fastest and easiest way to make them is with a kit. I use Tovolo Groovy Ice Pop Molds because they're BPA-free. I bought them on Amazon.com.

Cool tips

1 Although it doesn't add as much air as a commercial ice cream machine, your home ice cream maker does add air and volume.

2 To get a pretty scoop, you need to freeze your ice cream until it's hard, which means taking it from the ice cream machine to the freezer.

3 Let your homemade ice cream defrost for 10 to 20 minutes before scooping.

5 The more you thaw and refreeze your ice cream, the icier it will become.

4 The less sweetener you use, the harder your ice cream will freeze.

6 Keep an empty 6-cup rectangular glass storage dish in the freezer. That way, when you add freshly made ice cream, it won't melt as much.

Classic Flavors

28 Vanilla Ice Cream

30 Chocolate Ice Cream

32 Bing Cherry Ice Cream

34 Blueberry Lavender Ice Cream

36 Butter Pecan Ice Cream

38 Chocolate Hazelnut Ice Cream

40 Eggnog Ice Cream

42 Fig Ice Cream

44 Mint Chocolate Swirl Ice Cream

46 Pecan Praline Ice Cream

48 Piña Colada Ice Cream

50 Pistachio Ice Cream

52 Pumpkin Ice Cream

54 Fried Banana Ice Cream

56 Rocky Road Ice Cream

58 Rum Raisin Ice Cream

60 Saffron and Rose Ice Cream

62 Salted Caramel Chocolate Chunk Ice Cream

64 Strawberry Ice Cream

66 SunButter Fudge Ripple Ice Cream

68 Swiss Almond Ice Cream

70 Toasted Coconut Ice Cream

72 White Chocolate Goji Berry Ice Cream

Vanilla Ice Cream

I've never liked Vanilla Ice Cream on its own, but when it is combined with some mint extract, chocolate-covered almonds, or chocolate chip cookie dough, it's absolutely brilliant. You can also think of Vanilla Ice Cream as a canvas for your favorite toppings. The photograph on the opposite page shows just a few of the many possibilities: the top dish of Vanilla Ice Cream is topped with Ganache (page 176), warmed SunButter sauce (page 180), Whipped Coconut Cream (page 190), and freeze-dried strawberries; at the bottom left, the toppings shown are Strawberry Compote (page 186) and fresh fruit; and at the bottom right, Tart Cranberry Sauce (page 188) and walnuts.

---

1 (13.5-ounce) can full-fat coconut milk

½ cup (about 8) soft, pitted Medjool dates

1½ cups almond, cashew, or hemp milk

1 tablespoon vanilla extract

optional: thickener (page 19)

MAKES 1 TO 1½ QUARTS

1 Put the coconut milk and dates in a blender and purée until smooth.

2 Add the almond, cashew, or hemp milk, vanilla extract, and thickener (if using). Purée until smooth.

3 Freeze for about an hour or refrigerate until cold.

4 Pour into the ice cream machine and churn per the manufacturer's instructions.

5 Eat right away or freeze until hard for pretty scoops.

Chocolate Ice Cream

My Chocolate Ice Cream is extra creamy because I use dates and thickener. Mmm…

1 (13.5-ounce) can full-fat coconut milk

heaping ½ cup (about 10) soft, pitted Medjool dates

1 cup almond, cashew, or hemp milk

⅓ cup cocoa powder or raw cacao powder

1 tablespoon vanilla extract

optional: thickener (page 19)

MAKES 1 TO 1½ QUARTS

1   Put the coconut milk and dates in a blender and purée until smooth.

2   Add the almond, cashew, or hemp milk, cocoa powder or raw cacao powder, vanilla extract, and thickener (if using). Purée until smooth.

3   Freeze for about an hour or refrigerate until cold.

4   Pour into the ice cream machine and churn per the manufacturer's instructions.

5   Eat right away or freeze until hard for pretty scoops.

tip **Chocolate Ice Cream is one of my favorite flavors to eat in a Cookie Bowl. You can find that recipe on page 104.**

Bing Cherry Ice Cream

I have a passion for Bing cherries and cherry cordials. This ice cream combines those two flavors, making it one of my absolute favorites. When Bing cherries are in season, grab them for making ice cream, and add a little amaretto extract to really make it pop.

2 cups pitted Bing cherries, divided

1 (13.5-ounce) can full-fat coconut milk

½ cup (about 8) soft, pitted Medjool dates

1 cup almond, cashew, or hemp milk

1 teaspoon lemon juice

1 teaspoon vanilla extract

¼ teaspoon amaretto extract

optional: thickener (page 19)

MAKES 1 TO 1½ QUARTS

1   Put 1 cup of the pitted Bing cherries, coconut milk, and dates in a blender and purée until smooth.

2   Add the almond, cashew, or hemp milk, lemon juice, vanilla extract, amaretto extract, and thickener (if using). Purée until smooth.

3   Freeze for about an hour or refrigerate until cold.

4   Pour into the ice cream machine and churn per the manufacturer's instructions.

5   Finely chop the remaining 1 cup cherries, and add them to the ice cream when it reaches soft-serve consistency.

6   Eat right away or freeze until hard for pretty scoops.

Blueberry Lavender Ice Cream

This is one of those flavors that I had never heard of until one of my blog readers told me about it. Thank you so much—my family loves it! And the color is so pretty and fun.

1 cup fresh blueberries

1 (13.5-ounce) can full-fat coconut milk

½ cup (about 8) soft, pitted Medjool dates

½ teaspoon dried culinary lavender

1 cup almond, cashew, or hemp milk

1 teaspoon lemon juice

2 teaspoons vanilla extract

optional: thickener (page 19)

MAKES 1 TO 1½ QUARTS

1   Put the blueberries, coconut milk, dates, and lavender in a blender and purée until smooth.

2   Add the almond, cashew, or hemp milk, lemon juice, vanilla extract, and thickener (if using). Purée until smooth.

3   Freeze for about an hour or refrigerate until cold.

4   Pour into the ice cream machine and churn per the manufacturer's instructions.

5   Eat right away or freeze until hard for pretty scoops.

Butter Pecan Ice Cream

Butter pecan has always been one of my favorite flavors of ice cream. Who doesn't love anything buttery, really?

1½ cups pecan pieces

2 tablespoons plus ¼ cup buttery spread (page 19), divided

¼ teaspoon fine-grain sea salt

1 (13.5-ounce) can full-fat coconut milk

½ cup (about 8) soft, pitted Medjool dates

1¼ cups almond, cashew, or hemp milk

2 teaspoons vanilla extract

optional: thickener (page 19)

MAKES 1 TO 1½ QUARTS

1 Preheat the oven to 350°F. Spread the pecan pieces on a baking sheet and place in the oven for about 10 minutes, until lightly toasted.

2 Immediately put the toasted pecans in a mixing bowl along with 2 tablespoons of the buttery spread and the salt. Let the heat of the pecans melt the buttery spread. Stir to combine, then chill the nuts.

3 Put the remaining ¼ cup buttery spread, coconut milk, dates, almond, cashew, or hemp milk, vanilla extract, and thickener (if using) in a blender. Purée until smooth.

4 Freeze for about an hour or refrigerate until cold.

5 Pour into the ice cream machine and churn per the manufacturer's instructions.

6 Chop the pecans, and add them to the ice cream when it reaches soft-serve consistency.

7 Eat right away or freeze until hard for pretty scoops.

Chocolate Hazelnut Ice Cream

There are two ways to enjoy this flavor. For a chunky texture like Brownie Batter Ice Cream, you can add just a couple tablespoons of the Chocolate Hazelnut Spread to the Chocolate Ice Cream base, then fold in more spread before putting it in the freezer. Or, for a completely smooth ice cream, you can add a cup of the spread to the ice cream base and skip the folding. You can't go wrong either way.

1 batch Chocolate Ice Cream base
    (page 30)

1 cup Chocolate Hazelnut Spread
    (page 174)

MAKES 1 TO 1½ QUARTS

TO FOLD IN THE SPREAD

1   Make the Chocolate Ice Cream base. Add 2 tablespoons of the Chocolate Hazelnut Spread and purée until smooth.

2   Freeze for about an hour or refrigerate until cold.

3   Pour into the ice cream machine and churn per the manufacturer's instructions.

4   Transfer the ice cream to a 6-cup glass storage container, then fold in chunks of refrigerated Chocolate Hazelnut Spread.

5   Eat right away or freeze until hard for pretty scoops.

OR NOT TO FOLD

1   Make the Chocolate Ice Cream base, but omit the almond, cashew, or hemp milk. Add a cup of room-temperature Chocolate Hazelnut Spread and purée until smooth.

2   Freeze for about an hour or refrigerate until cold.

3   Pour into the ice cream machine and churn per the manufacturer's instructions.

4   Eat right away or freeze until hard for pretty scoops.

tip **Though you can use any cocoa powder to make chocolate ice cream, to get the rich, dark color shown in the photograph on the opposite page, you need to use black cocoa powder.**

Eggnog Ice Cream

We eat ice cream year-round. Making ice cream floats is a New Year's Eve tradition that my oldest daughter, Zoe, began a few years ago. For a new twist on the ice cream float, try adding Eggnog Ice Cream to chilled root beer.

1 batch Vanilla Ice Cream base (page 28)

2 teaspoons ground cinnamon

1 teaspoon nutmeg

¼ teaspoon allspice

MAKES 1 TO 1½ QUARTS

1   Make the Vanilla Ice Cream base. Add the cinnamon, nutmeg, and allspice and purée until smooth.

2   Freeze for about an hour or refrigerate until cold.

3   Pour into the ice cream machine and churn per the manufacturer's instructions.

4   Eat right away or freeze until hard for pretty scoops.

Fig Ice Cream

Dried figs give this ice cream a fantastic texture. I tried using soaked raw figs; however, figs are so much more amazing after being cooked slightly. If you're a fan of figs, you will love this ice cream. I like this flavor with thinned warmed SunButter (page 180) drizzled on top.

½ pound (about 18) organic dried figs

2 tablespoons buttery spread (page 19)

2 teaspoons lemon juice

1 (13.5-ounce) can full-fat coconut milk

1 cup almond, cashew, or hemp milk

2 tablespoons coconut sugar

1 tablespoon vanilla extract

big pinch of fine-grain sea salt

MAKES 1 TO 1½ QUARTS

1   Soak the figs in water for about 8 hours.

2   Drain the figs, discard the soaking water, remove the stems, and cut each fig in half.

3   In a medium saucepan over medium-low heat, combine the buttery spread, lemon juice, and figs. Cover and cook for about 10 minutes, stirring and mashing the figs down occasionally.

4   Put the cooked figs, coconut milk, almond, cashew, or hemp milk, coconut sugar, vanilla extract, and salt in a blender and purée until smooth.

5   Freeze for half an hour or refrigerate until cold.

6   Pour into the ice cream machine and churn per the manufacturer's instructions.

7   Eat right away or freeze until hard for pretty scoops.

Mint Chocolate Swirl Ice Cream

Mint chocolate chip was one of my two favorite ice cream flavors as a child. (The other was rocky road.) I gave it a twist by using a fudge swirl, and I think it's even better. If you prefer, you can add ½ cup dairy-free dark chocolate chips instead.

1 batch Vanilla Ice Cream base (page 28)

1 teaspoon alcohol-free mint extract or ½ teaspoon regular mint extract (with alcohol)

1 batch Ganache (page 176)

MAKES 1 TO 1½ QUARTS

1. Make the Vanilla Ice Cream base. Add the mint extract and purée until smooth.

2. Freeze for about an hour or refrigerate until cold.

3. Pour into the ice cream machine and churn per the manufacturer's instructions.

4. Transfer the ice cream to a 6-cup glass storage container, then fold in the Ganache.

5. Eat right away or freeze until hard for pretty scoops.

tip **To give this ice cream a green color, add a handful of fresh spinach and a teaspoon of lemon juice before puréeing. Even my kids can't taste the spinach in this mint ice cream.**

Pecan Praline Ice Cream

Candy-coated pecans are such a treat, especially when they are submerged in creamy ice cream.

2 tablespoons buttery spread (page 19)

2 tablespoons water

¾ cup plus 2 tablespoons coconut sugar, divided

2 cups pecans

1 (13.5-ounce) can full-fat coconut milk

1 cup almond, cashew, or hemp milk

1 teaspoon vanilla extract

optional: thickener (page 19)

MAKES 1 TO 1½ QUARTS

1   In a medium saucepan over medium-low heat, combine the buttery spread, water, ¾ cup of the coconut sugar, and pecans.

2   Simmer gently for 5 to 10 minutes, until the sugar is melted and slightly thickened.

3   Pour the candied pecans onto a sheet of unbleached parchment paper and set aside to cool.

4   Add ⅓ cup of the candied pecans, the remaining 2 tablespoons coconut sugar, coconut milk, almond, cashew, or hemp milk, vanilla extract, and thickener (if using) to a blender. Purée until smooth.

5   Freeze for about an hour or refrigerate until cold.

6   Pour into the ice cream machine and churn per the manufacturer's instructions.

7   Transfer the ice cream to a 6-cup glass storage container, then chop the rest of the candied pecans and fold them into the ice cream.

8   Eat right away or freeze until hard for pretty scoops.

Piña Colada Ice Cream

This tropical pineapple and coconut combination is great on a really hot summer day.

2½ cups coconut cream from packaged coconut milk (page 192) or fresh young coconuts (page 194)

¼ cup (about 4) soft, pitted Medjool dates

1¼ cups pineapple chunks

1 teaspoon vanilla extract

optional: 2 tablespoons white rum

MAKES 1 TO 1½ QUARTS

1 Put the coconut cream, dates, pineapple, vanilla extract, and rum (if using) in a blender or food processor and purée until smooth.

2 Freeze for about an hour or refrigerate until cold.

3 Pour into the ice cream machine and churn per the manufacturer's instructions.

4 Eat right away or freeze until hard for pretty scoops.

Pistachio Ice Cream

Pistachio was the first ice cream flavor I tested for this book. The girls loved it so much that I knew we were going to have a blast making the other flavors, too.

1 cup shelled, roasted, salted pistachios

½ cup raw honey or raw agave, heated slightly

1 (13.5-ounce) can full-fat coconut milk

1 cup almond, cashew, or hemp milk

1 tablespoon buttery spread (page 19)

1 teaspoon vanilla extract

optional: ¼ teaspoon almond extract

MAKES 1 TO 1½ QUARTS

1 Add the pistachios to a food processor fitted with an S-shaped blade. Purée until it has the consistency of a very fine meal.

2 Add the honey or agave to the food processor and purée until it is almost butter, scraping the sides as necessary while puréeing. Add some of the coconut milk if the mixture gets stuck.

3 Add the coconut milk, almond, cashew, or hemp milk, buttery spread, vanilla extract, and almond extract (if using). Purée until smooth.

4 Freeze for about an hour or refrigerate until cold.

5 Pour into the ice cream machine and churn per the manufacturer's instructions.

6 Eat right away or freeze until hard for pretty scoops.

Pumpkin Ice Cream

Have you ever had Pumpkin Ice Cream? We love to grow pumpkins (they're so easy to grow and fun to watch), which means that we end up making lots of pumpkin pie, pumpkin chili, and pumpkin granola (recipe on TheSpunkyCoconut.com). But Pumpkin Ice Cream is far easier to make, and it's so good.

1 (13.5-ounce) can full-fat coconut milk

½ cup (about 8) soft, pitted Medjool dates

1 cup almond, cashew, or hemp milk

1 cup pumpkin puree

1 teaspoon vanilla extract

2½ teaspoons ground cinnamon

½ teaspoon ground ginger

½ teaspoon nutmeg

⅛ teaspoon fine-grain sea salt

optional: thickener (page 19)

MAKES 1 TO 1½ QUARTS

1 Put the coconut milk and dates in a blender and purée until smooth.

2 Add the almond, cashew, or hemp milk, pumpkin puree, vanilla extract, cinnamon, ginger, nutmeg, salt, and thickener (if using). Purée until smooth.

3 Freeze for about an hour or refrigerate until cold.

4 Pour into the ice cream machine and churn per the manufacturer's instructions.

5 Eat right away or freeze until hard for pretty scoops.

tip **Just like pumpkin pie, I adore topping Pumpkin Ice Cream with Whipped Coconut Cream (page 190).**

Fried Banana Ice Cream

Fried bananas are amazing. They really make this flavor sing. If you've never made fried bananas, I really hope you'll give it a try.

2 tablespoons buttery spread (page 19)

2 ripe bananas, at room temperature

⅓ cup coconut sugar, finely ground in a spice grinder

1 (13.5-ounce) can full-fat coconut milk

2 tablespoons water

1 cup almond, cashew, or hemp milk

2 teaspoons vanilla extract

2 teaspoons lemon juice

big pinch of fine-grain sea salt

MAKES 1 TO 1½ QUARTS

1   Heat a 12-inch frying pan over medium heat, then add the buttery spread.

2   Slice the bananas into ½-inch pieces and lay them flat side down in the pan. Do not disturb them for 3 minutes.

3   Flip the bananas to the other side, and do not disturb them for another 3 minutes.

4   Put the browned bananas, ground coconut sugar, and coconut milk in a blender.

5   Wearing an oven mitt, add the water to the frying pan and swirl it around. This releases all the yummy brown bits on the bottom of the pan.

6   Add the pan water to the blender, then purée until smooth.

7   Add the almond, cashew, or hemp milk, vanilla extract, lemon juice, and salt. Purée until smooth.

8   Freeze for about an hour or refrigerate until cold.

9   Pour into the ice cream machine and churn per the manufacturer's instructions.

10 Eat right away or freeze until hard for pretty scoops.

Rocky Road Ice Cream

The chocolate ice cream, crunchy nuts, and gooey marshmallow cream were what I loved about rocky road as a child. And I still do.

1 cup walnuts, chopped

½ batch Chocolate Ice Cream base (page 30)

1 cup Honey Marshmallow Fluff (page 178) or Suzanne's Ricemellow Creme

MAKES 1 TO 1½ QUARTS

1 Preheat the oven to 350°F. Spread the walnuts on a baking sheet and place in the oven for about 10 minutes, until lightly toasted.

2 Make the Chocolate Ice Cream base.

3 Freeze for about 15 minutes or refrigerate until cold.

4 Pour into the ice cream machine and churn per the manufacturer's instructions.

5 Transfer the ice cream to a 6-cup glass storage container, then fold in the Honey Marshmallow Fluff and toasted walnuts.

6 Eat right away or freeze until hard for pretty scoops.

Rum Raisin Ice Cream

The first-ever cookbook devoted to ice cream was written by the French chef Monsieur Emy in 1768. Emy was opposed to alcohol as an ingredient, but he reluctantly made an exception for rum. Later, eighteenth- and nineteenth-century chefs enthusiastically embraced rum for their ice creams. (For more on the history of ice cream and nondairy ice cream, see pages 9 to 11.)

½ cup raisins

½ cup dark rum

1 batch Vanilla Ice Cream base (page 28)

MAKES 1 TO 1½ QUARTS

1   Soak the raisins in the rum for about 8 hours. Strain the raisins and reserve 2 tablespoons of the rum for the ice cream.

2   Make the Vanilla Ice Cream base. Add the reserved rum and purée until smooth.

3   Freeze for about an hour or refrigerate until cold.

4   Pour into the ice cream machine and churn per the manufacturer's instructions.

5   Add the raisins to the ice cream when it reaches soft-serve consistency.

6   Eat right away or freeze until hard for pretty scoops.

tip **This flavor is also nice with some nutmeg. Add nutmeg to your taste.**

Saffron and Rose Ice Cream

This ice cream is inspired by the Persian flavors of saffron and rose. Orange blossom water is also frequently used and is equally delicious if you can't find rose water.

1½ cups coconut cream, preferably from fresh young coconuts (page 194)

1½ cups canned full-fat coconut milk

about ¼ teaspoon saffron

½ cup (about 8) soft, pitted Medjool dates

½ cup almond, cashew, or hemp milk

1 teaspoon vanilla extract

1 tablespoon rose water

MAKES 1 TO 1½ QUARTS

1 Add the coconut cream, coconut milk, saffron, and dates to a food processor and purée until smooth.

2 Add the almond, cashew, or hemp milk, vanilla extract, and rose water. Purée until smooth.

3 Freeze for about an hour or refrigerate until cold.

4 Pour into the ice cream machine and churn per the manufacturer's instructions.

5 Eat right away or freeze until hard for pretty scoops.

Salted Caramel Chocolate Chunk Ice Cream

This recipe comes from my book *The Paleo Chocolate Lovers' Cookbook.* Salted caramel is one of the greatest things in the whole world. If you haven't tried it yet, you're going to love it.

1 batch Vanilla Ice Cream base (page 28)

1 batch Salted Caramel Sauce (page 184)

2 ounces dairy-free dark chocolate, chopped, or 1½ ounces cacao nibs

MAKES 1 TO 1½ QUARTS

1 Make the Vanilla Ice Cream base and purée until smooth.

2 Freeze for about an hour or refrigerate until cold.

3 Pour into the ice cream machine and churn per the manufacturer's instructions.

4 Transfer the ice cream to a 6-cup glass storage container, then fold in the Salted Caramel Sauce and chopped chocolate or cacao nibs.

5 Eat right away or freeze until hard for pretty scoops.

Strawberry Ice Cream

Strawberry ice cream is one of the most popular flavors among children. I know it's delicious and summery, but I can't help wonder: Is it the pink color that makes them so happy?

2 cups (about 10 ounces) fresh or frozen strawberries (see Tip)

1 (13.5-ounce) can full-fat coconut milk

½ cup (about 8) soft, pitted Medjool dates

½ cup almond, cashew, or hemp milk

1 teaspoon lemon juice

2 teaspoons vanilla extract

optional: thickener (page 19)

MAKES 1 TO 1½ QUARTS

1 Put the strawberries and coconut milk in a blender and purée until smooth.

2 Add the dates, almond, cashew, or hemp milk, lemon juice, vanilla extract, and thickener (if using). Purée until smooth.

3 Freeze for about an hour or refrigerate until cold (see Tip).

4 Pour into the ice cream machine and churn per the manufacturer's instructions.

5 Eat right away or freeze until hard for pretty scoops.

tip **If you use frozen strawberries, you can skip Step 3.**

SunButter Fudge Ripple Ice Cream

I prefer sunflower seeds to peanuts for health reasons. Peanuts, especially organic peanuts, carry a lot of mold. This SunButter Fudge Ripple is my version of peanut butter fudge ice cream, and it's completely delicious. I can't wait for you to try it!

1 (13.5-ounce) can full-fat coconut milk

½ cup (about 8) soft, pitted Medjool dates

1 cup sunflower seed butter, without added sugar or salt (see Tip)

½ cup water

1 tablespoon vanilla extract

2 teaspoons lemon juice

¼ teaspoon fine-grain sea salt

1 batch Ganache (page 176)

MAKES 1 TO 1½ QUARTS

1 Put all the ingredients except the Ganache in a food processor and purée until smooth.

2 Freeze for about an hour or refrigerate until cold.

3 Pour into the ice cream machine and churn per the manufacturer's instructions.

4 Transfer the ice cream to a 6-cup glass storage container, then fold in the Ganache.

5 Eat right away or freeze until hard for pretty scoops.

tip — **You can make your own sunflower seed butter by puréeing roasted, unsalted sunflower seeds in your food processor. Otherwise, I suggest the SunButter brand. The organic variety was free of added sugar at the time this book was published.**

Swiss Almond Ice Cream

Swiss Almond Ice Cream is so simple, but so satisfying. The contrast of sweet and salty, smooth and crunchy is what makes it so appealing.

1 cup whole raw almonds

½ cup dairy-free dark chocolate chips

¼ teaspoon fine-grain sea salt

1 batch Vanilla Ice Cream base (page 28)

¼ teaspoon almond extract

MAKES 1 TO 1½ QUARTS

1. Preheat the oven to 350°F.

2. Spread the almonds on a baking sheet and toast in the oven for about 12 minutes, until they are lightly browned, keeping a close eye on them to make sure they don't burn.

3. Put the toasted almonds in a mixing bowl along with the chocolate chips and salt. Cover and let sit for 3 minutes so that the heat from the almonds melts the chocolate.

4. Stir to coat the almonds with the chocolate and salt, then spread them on the lined baking sheet and chill in the refrigerator.

5. Make the Vanilla Ice Cream base. Add the almond extract and purée until smooth.

6. Freeze for about an hour or refrigerate until cold.

7. Pour into the ice cream machine and churn per the manufacturer's instructions.

8. Chop the coated nuts and set them aside.

9. Transfer the ice cream to a 6-cup glass storage container, then fold in the chopped coated nuts.

10. Eat right away or freeze until hard for pretty scoops.

Toasted Coconut Ice Cream

The difference between raw and toasted coconut is dramatic. Top this ice cream with Toasted Coconut Flakes (page 200) to add even more flavor.

1½ cups shredded unsweetened coconut

1½ (13.5-ounce) cans full-fat coconut milk, plus more as needed (see Tip)

½ cup (about 8) soft, pitted Medjool dates

1 tablespoon vanilla extract

big pinch of fine-grain sea salt

optional: thickener (page 19)

MAKES 1 TO 1½ QUARTS

1 Preheat the oven to 350°F. Spread the shredded coconut on a baking sheet and toast in the oven until it's nicely browned, about 12 minutes, stirring every few minutes and keeping a close eye on it so that it doesn't burn.

2 Add the toasted coconut and coconut milk to a medium-sized saucepan. Bring to a simmer over medium heat, watching carefully so that it doesn't boil over.

3 Turn off the heat, put the lid on the pan, and steep for 1 hour.

4 Pour the liquid over a fine-mesh strainer into a large mixing bowl. Press the shredded coconut down with a flexible silicone spatula to extract as much of the milk as possible.

5 Add the strained coconut milk to a blender along with the dates, vanilla extract, salt, and thickener (if using). Add more coconut milk as needed until you reach the 4-cup line on the blender. Purée until smooth.

6 Freeze for 30 minutes or refrigerate until cold.

7 Pour into the ice cream machine and churn per the manufacturer's instructions.

8 Eat right away or freeze until hard for pretty scoops.

tip **If you're up for the extra work, this ice cream is awesome with fresh puréed coconut meat. You can use it in place of the extra coconut milk in Step 5. Directions for opening a coconut are on page 194.**

White Chocolate Goji Berry Ice Cream

Packed with vitamins, minerals, protein, and antioxidants, goji berries are one of the most nutrient-dense fruits on the planet. Cacao butter contains powerful antioxidants and essential fatty acids. Not only that, but this ice cream is all about the flavor—dreamy white chocolate cacao butter and exotic berries. It's perfect for treating your sweetheart on Valentine's Day.

5 ounces raw cacao butter

1 cup dried goji berries, soaked in water for 20 minutes

1½ (13.5-ounce) cans full-fat coconut milk

½ cup (about 8) soft, pitted Medjool dates

little pinch of fine-grain sea salt

MAKES 1 TO 1½ QUARTS

1   Melt the cacao butter over a double boiler, then remove from the heat.

2   Strain the goji berries. Put the goji berries, melted cacao butter, coconut milk, dates, and salt in a blender or food processor and purée until smooth.

3   Freeze for no more than 30 minutes.

4   Pour into the ice cream machine and churn per the manufacturer's instructions.

5   Eat right away or freeze until hard for pretty scoops.

tip **This flavor takes much longer to soften before scooping because of the cacao butter. I recommend taking it out of the freezer 45 minutes before you plan to serve it. Or better yet, eat it right after making it.**

Coffee & Tea

Coffee Ice Cream

Using coffee as an ingredient is similar to cooking with wine: You have to use a good-quality coffee or wine for a nice end result. Our favorite coffee comes from Red Frog Coffee in Longmont, Colorado. It's roasted locally, organic, Fair Trade, and delicious.

½ cup whole coffee beans and 1 cup water (for a French press setup) or ¾ cup strong-brewed drip coffee

½ cup (about 8) soft, pitted Medjool dates

1½ (13.5-ounce) cans full-fat coconut milk

1 tablespoon vanilla extract

optional: thickener (page 19)

MAKES 1 TO 1½ QUARTS

1 If you're using a French press, grind the coffee beans and add them to the French press. Add the water, just off the boil, and steep for 10 minutes. Press the coffee grounds down, then pour the coffee into a blender. Or use ¾ cup strong-brewed drip coffee.

2 Add the dates to the blender and purée until smooth.

3 Add the coconut milk, vanilla extract, and thickener (if using) and purée until smooth.

4 Freeze for about an hour or refrigerate until cold.

5 Pour into the ice cream machine and churn per the manufacturer's instructions.

6 Eat right away or freeze until hard for pretty scoops.

Mocha Almond Fudge Ice Cream

1 batch Coffee Ice Cream base

1 cup Toasted Sliced Almonds (page 200)

1 batch Ganache (page 176)

1 Follow the Coffee Ice Cream directions through Step 5.

2 Transfer the ice cream to a 6-cup glass storage container, then fold in the Toasted Sliced Almonds and Ganache.

3 Eat right away or freeze until hard for pretty scoops.

Chai Ice Cream

Chai is my favorite hot tea, and it makes fabulous ice cream.

1 cup almond, cashew, or hemp milk

3 tablespoons plus 1 teaspoon loose-leaf chai black tea

½ cup (about 8) soft, pitted Medjool dates

1 (13.5-ounce) can full-fat coconut milk, plus more as needed (see Tip)

1 teaspoon vanilla extract

optional: thickener (page 19)

MAKES 1 TO 1½ QUARTS

1   Put the almond, cashew, or hemp milk in a small saucepan and bring to a simmer over medium heat.

2   Turn off the heat, add the chai tea, and steep for 20 minutes.

3   Pour the liquid over a fine-mesh strainer into a large measuring cup with a spout. Press down on the tea leaves to extract as much of the milk as possible.

4   Put the strained milk and dates in a blender and purée until smooth.

5   Add the coconut milk, vanilla extract, and thickener (if using). Add more coconut milk as needed until you reach the 4-cup line on the blender. Purée until smooth.

6   Freeze for about an hour or refrigerate until cold.

7   Pour into the ice cream machine and churn per the manufacturer's instructions.

8   Eat right away or freeze until hard for pretty scoops.

tip **For this and all other recipes that direct you to add more coconut milk until you reach the 4-cup line on the blender, you shouldn't need more than 1 additional can.**

Earl Grey Tea Ice Cream

When I decided to do a chapter on tea ice creams, I naively thought that each one would require the same amount of loose tea. This is not so. I ended up spending more time on each tea ice cream flavor than any of the other flavors in this book! It was all worth it, though, because we love them so much.

1 cup almond, cashew, or hemp milk

1 tablespoon plus 1 teaspoon loose-leaf Earl Grey tea

½ cup (about 8) soft, pitted Medjool dates

1 (13.5-ounce) can full-fat coconut milk, plus more as needed

1 teaspoon vanilla extract

optional: thickener (page 19)

MAKES 1 TO 1½ QUARTS

1   Put the almond, cashew, or hemp milk in a small saucepan, and bring to a simmer over medium heat.

2   Turn off the heat, add the Earl Grey tea, and steep for 20 minutes.

3   Pour the liquid over a fine-mesh strainer into a large measuring cup with a spout. Press down on the tea leaves to extract as much of the milk as possible.

4   Put the strained milk and dates in a blender and purée until smooth.

5   Add the coconut milk, vanilla extract, and thickener (if using). Add more coconut milk as needed until you reach the 4-cup line on the blender. Purée until smooth.

6   Freeze for about an hour or refrigerate until cold.

7   Pour into the ice cream machine and churn per the manufacturer's instructions.

8   Eat right away or freeze until hard for pretty scoops.

Ginger Kombucha Tea Ice Cream

There are instructions for making your own kombucha on my blog (TheSpunkyCoconut.com), and store-bought kombucha has become widely available. Ginger kombucha is my family's favorite flavor, but if you're not in the mood for ginger, substitute whatever kombucha flavor sounds good to you and omit the fresh ginger.

1½ cups ginger kombucha

½ cup (about 8) soft, pitted Medjool dates

1 to 2 inches fresh peeled ginger root, to taste

1 (13.5-ounce) can full-fat coconut milk

1 teaspoon vanilla extract

optional: thickener (page 19)

MAKES 1 TO 1½ QUARTS

1   Pour the kombucha into a blender, add the dates and ginger root, and purée until smooth.

2   Add the coconut milk, vanilla extract, and thickener (if using) and purée until smooth.

3   Freeze for about an hour or refrigerate until cold.

4   Pour into the ice cream machine and churn per the manufacturer's instructions.

5   Eat right away or freeze until hard for pretty scoops.

Honeysuckle Ice Cream

Have you ever pulled apart a honeysuckle and tasted the nectar inside? My dear friend Emily and I used to do this in Maryland when we were little girls.

2 heaping tablespoons honeysuckle flower strands

1 cup water, just off the boil

½ cup (about 8) soft, pitted Medjool dates

1 (13.5-ounce) can full-fat coconut milk, plus more as needed

1 teaspoon vanilla extract

optional: thickener (page 19)

MAKES 1 TO 1½ QUARTS

1 Place the honeysuckle strands in a small bowl. Pour the hot water over the honeysuckle strands, and steep for about 20 minutes.

2 Pour the liquid over a fine-mesh strainer into a large measuring cup with a spout.

3 Put the strained liquid and the dates in a blender and purée until smooth.

4 Add the coconut milk, vanilla extract, and thickener (if using). Add more coconut milk as needed until you reach the 4-cup line on the blender. Purée until smooth.

5 Freeze for about an hour or refrigerate until cold.

6 Pour into the ice cream machine and churn per the manufacturer's instructions.

7 Eat right away or freeze until hard for pretty scoops.

tip **Honeysuckle is thought to be one of the most important herbs for liver detoxification.**

Jasmine Tea Ice Cream

Jasmine is one of the best scents in the world, isn't it? Whenever I'm in a boutique gift shop, I can always be found standing by the jasmine soaps, inhaling deeply with a bar against my nose. This ice cream tastes pretty, like jasmine, if that makes any sense.

1 cup almond, cashew, or hemp milk

3 tablespoons loose-leaf jasmine tea

½ cup (about 8) soft, pitted Medjool dates

1 (13.5-ounce) can full-fat coconut milk, plus more as needed

1 teaspoon vanilla extract

optional: thickener (page 19)

MAKES 1 TO 1½ QUARTS

1   Put the almond, cashew, or hemp milk in a small saucepan, and bring to a simmer over medium heat.

2   Turn off the heat, add the jasmine tea, and steep for 20 minutes.

3   Pour the liquid over a fine-mesh strainer into a large measuring cup with a spout. Press down on the tea leaves to extract as much of the milk as possible.

4   Put the strained milk and dates in a blender and purée until smooth.

5   Add the coconut milk, vanilla extract, and thickener (if using). Add more coconut milk as needed until you reach the 4-cup line on the blender. Purée until smooth.

6   Freeze for about an hour or refrigerate until cold.

7   Pour into the ice cream machine and churn per the manufacturer's instructions.

8   Eat right away or freeze until hard for pretty scoops.

tip **Because toasted coconut and jasmine go so well together, I always top this ice cream with toasted coconut. The recipe for Toasted Coconut Flakes is on page 200.**

Matcha Ice Cream

Matcha is a Japanese green tea that has an ultra-fine powdery texture. It has great flavor and color, plus it's full of antioxidants, vitamins, and minerals. And it is really fun to use in ice cream (and in truffles—see my cookbook *The Paleo Chocolate Lovers' Cookbook*).

1 cup almond, cashew, or hemp milk

1 tablespoon matcha powder

½ cup (about 8) soft, pitted Medjool dates

1½ (13.5-ounce) cans full-fat coconut milk

1 teaspoon vanilla extract

optional: thickener (page 19)

MAKES 1 TO 1½ QUARTS

1. Put the almond, cashew, or hemp milk in a small saucepan, and bring to a simmer over medium heat.

2. Turn off the heat, add the matcha powder, and steep for 20 minutes.

3. Put the steeped milk and dates in a blender and purée until smooth. (Matcha powder does not need to be strained like other teas.)

4. Add the coconut milk, vanilla extract, and thickener (if using). Purée until smooth.

5. Freeze for about an hour or refrigerate until cold.

6. Pour into the ice cream machine and churn per the manufacturer's instructions.

7. Eat right away or freeze until hard for pretty scoops.

Rooibos Tea Ice Cream

If you like chai, then you should give rooibos tea a try. The flavor is different, but both teas are rich and satisfying.

1 cup almond, cashew, or hemp milk

3 tablespoons loose-leaf rooibos tea

½ cup (about 8) soft, pitted Medjool dates

1 (13.5-ounce) can full-fat coconut milk, plus more as needed

1 teaspoon vanilla extract

optional: thickener (page 19)

MAKES 1 TO 1½ QUARTS

1   Put the almond, cashew, or hemp milk in a small saucepan, and bring to a simmer over medium heat.

2   Turn off the heat, add the rooibos tea, and steep for 20 minutes.

3   Pour the liquid over a fine-mesh strainer into a large measuring cup with a spout. Press down on the tea leaves to extract as much of the milk as possible.

4   Put the strained milk and dates in a blender and purée until smooth.

5   Add the coconut milk, vanilla extract, and thickener (if using). Add more coconut milk as needed until you reach the 4-cup line on the blender. Purée until smooth.

6   Freeze for about an hour or refrigerate until cold.

7   Pour into the ice cream machine and churn per the manufacturer's instructions.

8   Eat right away or freeze until hard for pretty scoops.

Mulled Cider Ice Cream

Mulled Cider Ice Cream is a great treat to enjoy in the fall. Apples, cinnamon, cloves, orange peel, and star anise impart the flavor of mulled cider, but with the added creaminess of ice cream.

1½ cups cider, with no added sweetener

2 heaping tablespoons mulling spices

½ cup (about 8) soft, pitted Medjool dates

1 (13.5-ounce) can full-fat coconut milk, plus more as needed

1 teaspoon vanilla extract

optional: thickener (page 19)

optional: about 1/4 teaspoon natural yellow food coloring (see Tip)

MAKES 1 TO 1½ QUARTS

1 Combine the cider and mulling spices in a small heavy-bottomed saucepan and simmer over low heat for 20 minutes.

2 Let the cider cool, then pour over a fine-mesh strainer into a large measuring cup with a spout.

3 Put the strained cider and dates in a blender and purée until smooth.

4 Add the coconut milk, vanilla extract, thickener (if using), and food coloring (if using). Add more coconut milk as needed until you reach the 4-cup line on the blender. Purée until smooth.

5 Freeze for about an hour or refrigerate until cold.

6 Pour into the ice cream machine and churn per the manufacturer's instructions.

7 Eat right away or freeze until hard for pretty scoops.

 The ice cream pictured in the photo at right does include the optional yellow food coloring.

Frozen Coffee or Tea Latte

The Frozen Tea Latte in this photo is made with chai. I chose it for the picture because of its gorgeous brown color. Half the fun of taking the photo is devouring the ice cream afterward.

1 batch Coffee Ice Cream (page 76) or tea-flavored ice cream of your choice (pages 78 to 90)

1 batch Whipped Coconut Cream (page 190)

MAKES 4 (8-OUNCE) SERVINGS

1 Make the Coffee Ice Cream or tea-flavored ice cream.

2 Freeze for about an hour or refrigerate until cold.

3 Pour into the ice cream machine and churn per the manufacturer's instructions.

4 When the ice cream reaches soft-serve consistency, turn the machine off, divide the ice cream among 4 glasses, and top with Whipped Coconut Cream.

Cakes & Cookies

Brownies à la Mode

I love Brownies à la Mode, so I tweaked my most popular brownie recipe for this book. These brownies are dense and fudgy, like great brownies should be.

DRY INGREDIENTS

1 tablespoon flax meal

½ teaspoon baking soda

¼ teaspoon fine-grain sea salt

½ cup coconut sugar

¼ cup plus 3 tablespoons cocoa powder

1 tablespoon coconut flour, sifted

WET INGREDIENTS

¼ cup plus 2 tablespoons water

¼ cup melted buttery spread (page 19), plus extra for greasing the pan

1 cup almond butter (I prefer raw, but roasted also works)

MAKES 8 BROWNIES

1 Preheat the oven to 350°F. Grease an 8-by-8-inch baking dish.

2 In a medium mixing bowl, whisk together the dry ingredients.

3 In a large mixing bowl, combine the wet ingredients with an electric mixer.

4 Add the dry ingredients to the wet ingredients and mix with an electric mixer until smooth.

5 Transfer the batter to the greased baking dish and use a flexible silicone spatula to spread it evenly.

6 Bake for 30 minutes or until a knife inserted into the middle comes out mostly clean.

7 Let the brownies cool in the pan on the counter, then refrigerate to set.

8 Serve with a scoop of ice cream on top.

(tip) **For a nut-free version, substitute sunflower seed butter (SunButter), double the salt, and omit the baking soda. Be aware, however, that sunflower seed butter reacts with baking soda and turns green. Although it's perfectly harmless, it isn't very appetizing.**

Brownie Batter Ice Cream

From college until my mid-twenties (when I stopped eating dairy), brownie batter was my favorite ice cream flavor. I'm still a huge fan of eating brownie batter in general, and this ice cream flavor might be the best one in the book, in my opinion.

1 batch Chocolate Ice Cream base (page 30)

1 batch Brownie Batter (recipe follows)

MAKES 1 TO 1½ QUARTS

1 Make the Chocolate Ice Cream base.

2 Freeze for about an hour or refrigerate until cold.

3 Pour into the ice cream machine and churn per the manufacturer's instructions.

4 Transfer the ice cream to a 6-cup glass storage container, then fold in the Brownie Batter.

5 Eat right away or freeze until hard for pretty scoops.

Brownie Batter

½ cup water

1 cup almond butter (I prefer raw, but roasted also works)

½ cup cocoa powder or raw cacao powder

¼ cup coconut sugar, ground in a spice grinder

⅛ teaspoon vanilla liquid stevia (or more coconut sugar, to taste)

½ teaspoon fine-grain sea salt

1 In a mixing bowl, mix all the ingredients together with an electric mixer until smooth.

2 Use the batter for folding into Chocolate Ice Cream.

 You can substitute sunflower seed butter (SunButter) if you cannot tolerate almonds.

Carrot Cake Ice Cream

I'm crazy about carrot cake. If I could eat only one kind of cake ever again, I would choose carrot cake. It only makes sense that I love this Carrot Cake Ice Cream, too.

about 4 carrots

1 (13.5-ounce) can full-fat coconut milk

½ cup almond, cashew, or hemp milk

½ cup (about 8) soft, pitted Medjool dates

1 teaspoon vanilla extract

2 teaspoons ground cinnamon

¼ teaspoon ground allspice

big pinch of fine-grain sea salt

optional: thickener (page 19)

1 cup raisins

1 cup walnuts, chopped

MAKES 1 TO 1½ QUARTS

1 Chop the carrots into roughly ½-inch pieces until you have about 2 cups' worth.

2 Steam the carrots until they are fork tender (about 10 minutes), then drain.

3 Put the steamed carrots, coconut milk, almond, cashew, or hemp milk, dates, vanilla extract, cinnamon, allspice, salt, and thickener (if using) in a blender. Purée until smooth.

4 Freeze for about an hour or refrigerate until cold.

5 Pour into the ice cream machine and churn per the manufacturer's instructions.

6 Transfer the ice cream to a 6-cup glass storage container, then fold in the raisins and walnuts.

7 Eat right away or freeze until hard for pretty scoops.

Cookie Bowls

I looked into getting an ice cream cone maker and discovered that they cost fifty dollars. So, rather than recommend one more appliance, I created these cookie bowls using small ramekins, which cost one dollar each.

¼ cup golden flax meal

¾ cup almond flour, plus more for rolling the dough

1 tablespoon arrowroot flour

2 tablespoons coconut sugar, ground in a spice grinder

⅛ teaspoon fine-grain sea salt

½ teaspoon melted coconut oil

⅓ cup water, just off the boil

MAKES 4 BOWLS

1   Preheat the oven to 350°F.

2   In a mixing bowl, whisk together the golden flax meal, almond flour, arrowroot flour, coconut sugar, and salt until evenly combined.

3   Add the melted coconut oil and hot water to the flour mixture. Use an electric mixer to combine until it looks like dough, then let the dough rest for 5 minutes. The dough will be very sticky—that's how it's supposed to be.

4   Divide the dough into 4 pieces. Place each piece on a sheet of unbleached parchment paper.

5   Roll each piece of dough into a 6-inch circle, sprinkling the top of the dough with almond flour as needed to prevent sticking.

6   Do not try to remove the parchment paper from underneath the dough. Use scissors to trim the paper close to the edge of the dough.

7   Lay each circle of dough over a small (6-ounce/3½-inch) oven-safe ramekin turned upside down on a cookie sheet.

8   Make 8 pinches around the bottom edge of each circle so that the cookie dough drapes like a ball gown.

9   Bake for 40 minutes, then turn the oven off and leave them in for 40 more minutes.

10   Remove the bowls from the ramekins and turn them over. The paper will come off easily. Place a cookie bowl on a plate and fill with ice cream.

note **These yummy Cookie Bowls will stay crunchy even when the ice cream has melted!**

Chocolate Chip Cookies

These cookies are from my book *The Paleo Chocolate Lovers' Cookbook.*

2 cups almond flour

¼ cup arrowroot flour

½ cup coconut sugar

½ teaspoon fine-grain sea salt

¼ teaspoon baking soda

½ cup dairy-free dark chocolate chips

½ cup palm shortening

1 teaspoon vanilla extract

splash of water

MAKES 20 COOKIES

1 Preheat the oven to 350°F. Line a cookie sheet with unbleached parchment paper.

2 In a mixing bowl, whisk together the almond flour, arrowroot flour, coconut sugar, salt, baking soda, and chocolate chips until evenly combined.

3 Add the palm shortening, vanilla extract, and water to the flour mixture, then mix with an electric mixer for about 10 seconds.

4 Pack the dough into a 1½-tablespoon (size 40) scoop with a lever, and level it off. Then use the lever to place the ball of dough on the lined cookie sheet. Repeat with the remaining dough.

5 Wet your hands and use your palms to flatten each ball to about 2 inches wide. Leave about 2 inches of space between the flattened cookies.

6 Bake the cookies for about 12 minutes, or until the edges are nicely golden.

7 Let the cookies cool on the cookie sheet for 5 minutes before using a spatula to transfer them to wire racks to cool completely.

Chocolate Chip Cookie Dough Ice Cream

I like my Chocolate Chip Cookie Dough Ice Cream to be full of cookie dough. That always bothered me about the store-bought versions—there was never enough cookie dough.

1 batch Vanilla Ice Cream base (page 28)

1 batch Chocolate Chip Cookie dough (use the recipe for Chocolate Chip Cookies, page 106)

MAKES 1 TO 1½ QUARTS

1 Make the Vanilla Ice Cream base.

2 Freeze for about an hour or refrigerate until cold.

3 While the base is chilling, make the Chocolate Chip Cookie dough. Roll the cookie dough into little balls and refrigerate them until the ice cream is ready.

4 Pour the base into the ice cream machine and churn per the manufacturer's instructions.

5 Transfer the ice cream to a 6-cup glass storage container, then fold in little balls of cookie dough.

6 Eat right away or freeze until hard for pretty scoops.

tip **I like to save some of the cookie dough for topping and some for baking, but you can put as much in the ice cream as you like.**

Chocolate Chip Ice Cream Sandwiches

1 batch Vanilla Ice Cream (page 28)

Chocolate Chip Cookies (page 106)

MAKES 10 SANDWICHES

1 Make the Vanilla Ice Cream as directed, and put the dish of ice cream in the freezer to harden further—until it is just scoopable, not rock hard.

2 Make the Chocolate Chip Cookies, then put them in the freezer with parchment paper between them so that they don't stick together. Freezing the cookies makes the sandwiches easier to assemble.

3 When the ice cream reaches scooping temperature, add a scoop to the back side of a cookie. Press another cookie on top. Repeat the process with the rest of the cookies.

4 Freeze the ice cream sandwiches until they are set. If they are frozen solid, let them thaw for about 15 minutes before serving.

Frozen Mint Chocolate Whoopie Pies

1 batch Chocolate Ice Cream (page 30)

1 batch Chocolate Whoopie Pie Cakes
(recipe follows)

MAKES 5 WHOOPIE PIES

1   Make the Chocolate Ice Cream as directed. Put the dish of ice cream in the freezer to harden further—until it is just scoopable, not rock hard.

2   Make the Chocolate Whoopie Pie Cakes, then put them in the freezer with parchment paper between them so that they don't stick together. Freezing the cakes makes the sandwiches easier to assemble.

3   When the ice cream reaches scooping temperature, add a scoop to the back side of a cake. Press another cake on top. Repeat the process with the rest of the cakes.

4   Freeze the ice cream sandwiches until they are set. If they are frozen solid, let them thaw for about 15 minutes before serving.

Chocolate Whoopie Pie Cakes

You can make these Whoopie Pie Cakes without the mint extract or even substitute another extract, like almond or amaretto.

DRY INGREDIENTS
½ cup coconut sugar
¼ cup flax meal
½ cup cocoa powder
½ cup coconut flour, sifted
¼ cup arrowroot flour
1 teaspoon baking soda

WET INGREDIENTS
1 cup canned full-fat coconut milk
½ cup applesauce with no added sugar
¼ teaspoon vanilla liquid stevia
¼ cup melted coconut oil
optional: 1 teaspoon alcohol-free mint extract or ½ teaspoon regular mint extract (with alcohol)

MAKES 10 CAKES

1. Preheat the oven to 325°F. Line a cookie sheet with unbleached parchment paper.

2. In a medium mixing bowl, whisk together the dry ingredients.

3. In a large mixing bowl, use an electric mixer to combine the wet ingredients, adding the melted coconut oil last, while the mixer is on. (If you are making Frozen Mint Chocolate Whoopie Pies, add the optional mint extract to the wet ingredients as well.)

4. Add the dry ingredients to the wet ingredients and combine with an electric mixer until smooth.

5. Pack the dough into a large (⅓-cup/size 12) ice cream scoop with a lever, and level it off. Use the lever to transfer each scoop to the lined cookie sheet, spacing the scoops about 3 inches apart.

6. Use wet hands to flatten the scoops to about 3-inch circles.

7. Bake the cakes for about 25 minutes, until they spring back slightly when touched. Let them cool on the sheet for about 5 minutes, then transfer them to wire racks to cool completely.

tip **This cake batter, which is more like dough, is the perfect consistency for making whoopie pies. It also works really well for ice cream cakes like Mini Strawberry Ice Cream Cakes with Chocolate Crackle (page 124) and Fried Banana and Chocolate Ice Cream Cake (page 116).**

Fried Banana and Chocolate Ice Cream Cake

Over Christmas we had a blast when my mom came to visit us in California. We brainstormed ideas for ice cream cakes while driving to the beach. The idea for this fabulous flavor combination was all hers.

1 batch Fried Banana Ice Cream
    (page 54)

1 batch Chocolate Whoopie Pie Cakes
    (page 114)

1½ ounces dairy-free dark chocolate

¼ cup canned full-fat coconut milk

bananas to garnish

SERVES 12 TO 16

1   Make the Fried Banana Ice Cream as directed. Put the dish of ice cream in the freezer to harden further—until it is just scoopable, not rock hard.

2   Preheat the oven to 325°F, then make the dough for the Chocolate Whoopie Pie Cakes.

3   Line the bottoms of two 7-inch springform pans with unbleached parchment paper, then divide the dough evenly between the pans. Use a flexible silicone spatula to spread the dough evenly and pack it down.

4   Bake the cakes for about 40 minutes. Let cool, then remove from the pans.

5   Trim the edges of the cakes with a serrated knife to make them straight. Wrap each cake in parchment paper, then freeze. (This makes the cake easier to assemble.)

6   When the ice cream reaches scooping temperature, spread half evenly onto the first cake.

7   Gently press the other cake on top of the ice cream. Add the other half of the ice cream to the top of the second cake, and spread evenly.

8   Quickly place banana slices on top of the ice cream, then freeze the cake for at least 8 hours.

9   Heat the chocolate and coconut milk over a double boiler until just melted. Remove from the heat and let cool to room temperature.

10 Transfer the chocolate to one corner of a plastic food storage bag, then snip about ⅛ inch off the tip.

11 Pipe the chocolate back and forth across the top of the ice cream cake. Turn the cake 90 degrees and repeat the piping, creating a lattice-like effect.

12 Allow the cake to sit at room temperature for about an hour before slicing.

Gingerbread Cookies

This is a variation of my most popular gingerbread cookie recipe. I love how the following two recipes that use this cookie are so appropriate for the fall.

3 tablespoons flax meal

½ cup coconut sugar, ground in a spice grinder

1 cup almond flour

½ cup coconut flour, sifted

1 teaspoon baking soda

2 teaspoons ground cinnamon

2 teaspoons ground ginger

¼ teaspoon ground allspice

⅛ teaspoon vanilla liquid stevia

½ cup applesauce with no added sugar

1 teaspoon vanilla extract

¼ cup melted coconut oil

MAKES 16 COOKIES

1   Preheat the oven to 350°F. Line a cookie sheet with unbleached parchment paper.

2   In a mixing bowl, whisk together the flax meal, coconut sugar, almond flour, coconut flour, baking soda, cinnamon, ginger, and allspice.

3   Add the liquid stevia, applesauce, and vanilla extract to the flour mixture, and begin to combine it with an electric mixer. Add the melted coconut oil last, while the mixer is running. Continue mixing for about 10 seconds.

4   Pack the dough into a 1½-tablespoon (size 40) scoop with a lever, and level it off. Then use the lever to place the ball of dough on the lined cookie sheet. Repeat with the remaining dough.

5   Wet your hands and use your palms to flatten each ball to about 2 inches wide. The cookies will not spread in the oven.

6   Bake the cookies for about 18 minutes, or until the edges are beginning to crisp.

7   Let the cookies cool on the cookie sheet for 5 minutes before using a spatula to transfer them to wire racks to cool completely.

Gingerbread Cookie Dough Ice Cream

The more cookie dough the merrier, and this one is great for the holidays.

1 batch Vanilla Ice Cream base (page 28)

1 batch Gingerbread Cookie dough (use the recipe for Gingerbread Cookies, page 118)

MAKES 1 TO 1½ QUARTS

1   Make the Vanilla Ice Cream base.

2   Freeze for about an hour or refrigerate until cold.

3   While the base is chilling, make the Gingerbread Cookie dough. Roll the cookie dough into little balls and refrigerate them until the ice cream is ready.

4   Pour the base into the ice cream machine and churn per the manufacturer's instructions.

5   Transfer the ice cream to a 6-cup glass storage container, then fold in little balls of cookie dough.

6   Eat right away or freeze until hard for pretty scoops.

tip I like to save some of the cookie dough for topping and some for baking, but you can put as much in the ice cream as you like.

Gingerbread Ice Cream Sandwiches

The idea to combine Gingerbread Cookies and Carrot Cake Ice Cream to make sandwiches came from one of my amazing editors. Thank you—we love it!

1 batch Carrot Cake Ice Cream (page 102)

1 batch Gingerbread Cookies (page 118)

MAKES 8 SANDWICHES

1 Make the Carrot Cake Ice Cream as directed, and put the dish of ice cream in the freezer to harden further—until it is just scoopable, not rock hard.

2 Make the Gingerbread Cookies, then put them in the freezer with parchment paper between them so that they don't stick together. Freezing the cookies makes the sandwiches easier to assemble.

3 When the ice cream reaches scooping temperature, add a scoop to the back side of a cookie. Press another cookie on top. Repeat the process with the rest of the cookies.

4 Freeze the ice cream sandwiches until they are set. If they are frozen solid, let them thaw for about 15 minutes before serving.

Mini Strawberry Ice Cream Cakes with Chocolate Crackle

With one batch each of Strawberry Ice Cream, Chocolate Whoopie Pie Cakes, and Chocolate Crackle, you can make three of these adorable mini ice cream cakes.

1 batch Strawberry Ice Cream (page 64)

1 batch Chocolate Whoopie Pie Cakes (page 114)

1 batch Chocolate Crackle (page 172)

special equipment: 3 (4.7- or 6-inch) disposable paper Bundt pans (see Tip)

MAKES 3 MINI CAKES

1 Make the Strawberry Ice Cream as directed. Put the dish of ice cream in the freezer to harden further—until it is just scoopable, not rock hard.

2 Preheat the oven to 325°F, then make the dough for the Chocolate Whoopie Pie Cakes.

3 Divide the dough evenly among three (4.7- or 6-inch diameter) paper Bundt pans. Use a flexible silicone spatula to press the dough down firmly and smooth the tops.

4 Bake the cakes on a baking sheet for about 40 minutes, or until a knife inserted comes out mostly clean.

5 Let the cakes cool on the counter, then freeze them for about 30 minutes.

6 Add the Strawberry Ice Cream to the tops of the cakes. It's easiest if the ice cream is pretty soft.

7 Freeze the ice cream cakes overnight.

8 To serve the cakes, let them thaw for about 15 minutes, then carefully peel off all the paper. Pour the Chocolate Crackle over the cakes, then slice when the cakes are soft enough (about another 15 minutes).

tip

Make sure that the sides of the cake pans are straight if you want the ice cream layer on top. If the sides are angled, you will want to flip the cakes over to serve them.

Little paper Bundt pans are made by the Welcome Home company and can be found on Amazon.com. They are made by other companies as well and can be found at stores like World Market and Ace Hardware.

Mint Whipped Cream Bites

I don't know when round bites of ice cream coated in chocolate first came to be, but I do remember seeing commercials for them when I was growing up. We called them bonbons. Whatever you call them, these little guys are so much fun to eat.

2 cups Whipped Coconut Cream (page 190)

2 tablespoons raw honey or raw agave

¾ teaspoon mint extract

⅛ teaspoon vanilla liquid stevia

optional: several drops natural yellow and blue food coloring

1 batch Chocolate Crackle (page 172)

special equipment: Medium Classic Round Truffle Mold from Truffly Made

MAKES ABOUT 35 (1-INCH-ROUND) BITES

1. In a small bowl, use an electric mixer to combine the Whipped Coconut Cream with the honey or agave, mint extract, liquid stevia, and food coloring (if using).

2. Transfer the filling to one corner of a large plastic food storage bag, and snip about ¼ inch off the tip.

3. Squeeze the air out of the bag, and pipe the filling into the cavities in the truffle mold. (You should have enough filling to fill approximately 35 of the cavities.) Freeze until hard.

4. Pop the filling balls out of the molds, and return them to the freezer.

5. Make the Chocolate Crackle. Pour the chocolate into a small heatproof or glass bowl (I use a mason jar), and allow it to come to room temperature. The chocolate won't harden until it meets the frozen cream.

6. Place a piece of unbleached parchment paper on a baking sheet. This is where the bites will dry after you coat them in the chocolate.

7. Take out about 5 frozen filling balls at a time, keeping the rest in the freezer so that they don't melt while you're coating them.

8. Use a toothpick inserted at an angle into the bottom to dip each ball into the chocolate.

9. Let the coating harden, twisting the toothpick between your fingers. (This takes only a few seconds.)

10. Dip each ball a second time, and set them on the lined baking sheet to dry, leaving the toothpicks in place.

11. When dry, ease the bites off the toothpicks by pulling against the surface while pressing gently with your index finger.

12. Store the bites in the freezer, and let them defrost on the counter for about 20 minutes before serving.

N'oatmeal Cookie Ice Cream Sandwiches

1 batch Vanilla Ice Cream (page 28)

1 batch N'oatmeal Cookies (recipe follows)

MAKES 11 SANDWICHES

1 Make the Vanilla Ice Cream as directed. Put the dish of ice cream in the freezer to harden further—until it is just scoopable, not rock hard.

2 Make the N'oatmeal Cookies, then put them in the freezer with parchment paper between them so that they don't stick together. Freezing the cookies makes the sandwiches easier to assemble.

3 When the ice cream reaches scooping temperature, add a scoop to the back side of a cookie. Press another cookie on top. Repeat the process with the rest of the cookies.

4 Freeze the ice cream sandwiches until they are set. If they are frozen solid, let them thaw for about 15 minutes before serving.

N'oatmeal Cookies

¾ cup raisins

½ cup shredded unsweetened coconut

¼ cup flax meal

2 teaspoons ground cinnamon

¼ teaspoon ground allspice

¼ teaspoon fine-grain sea salt

¼ teaspoon baking soda

1 cup almond butter

⅓ cup water

2 tablespoons raw honey or raw agave

⅛ teaspoon vanilla liquid stevia

MAKES ABOUT 22 COOKIES

1 Preheat the oven to 350°F. Line a cookie sheet with unbleached parchment paper.

2 In a mixing bowl, whisk together the raisins, coconut, flax meal, cinnamon, allspice, salt, and baking soda until combined.

3 Add the almond butter, water, honey or agave, and liquid stevia. Combine with an electric mixer for about 10 seconds.

4 Use a 1½-tablespoon (size 40) scoop with a lever to transfer the dough to a cookie sheet lined with unbleached parchment paper. (Or use a spoon to make 22 drops of dough.)

5 Wet your hands and use your palms to flatten each cookie to the desired thickness. Leave an inch of space between the flattened cookies.

6 Bake for about 15 minutes, or until slightly golden. Let the cookies cool on the cookie sheet for 5 minutes before using a spatula to transfer them to wire racks to cool completely.

"Peanut Butter" Chocolate Ice Cream Cake

This "Peanut Butter" Chocolate Ice Cream Cake may look complicated, but it really doesn't take any longer than a frosted cake to make.

1 cup salted, roasted sunflower seeds

¼ cup (about 4) soft, pitted Medjool dates

½ teaspoon ground cinnamon

1 batch SunButter Fudge Ripple Ice Cream (ganache omitted) (page 66)

1½ ounces dairy-free dark chocolate

¼ cup canned full-fat coconut milk

SERVES 12

1 To make the crust, place the sunflower seeds, dates, and cinnamon in a food processor fitted with an S-shaped blade. Pulse to create a very fine meal.

2 Line the bottom of a 7-inch springform pan with unbleached parchment paper, then press the crust evenly on top. Set aside.

3 Rinse the food processor, then use it to make the SunButter Fudge Ripple Ice Cream, minus the ganache (fudge ripple).

4 Pour the ice cream puree over the prepared crust and freeze for at least 8 hours.

5 Heat the chocolate and coconut milk over a double boiler until just melted. Remove from the heat and let cool to room temperature.

6 Transfer the chocolate to one corner of a plastic food storage bag, then snip about ⅛ inch off the tip.

7 Pipe the chocolate back and forth across the top of the cake. Turn the cake 90 degrees and repeat the piping, creating a lattice-like effect.

8 Allow the cake to sit at room temperature for about an hour before slicing.

Yogurt, Pops, & Sherbet

Yummy Yogurt Drink

I am obsessed with my dairy-free Yogurt Drink. I make it constantly. All you do is simmer your "milk," allow it to cool, whisk in probiotics, and let it ferment. The good bacteria will eat the sugar to grow, and you are left with a yogurt that has the consistency of a milkshake. It's so easy!

2 (13.5-ounce) cans full-fat coconut milk

4 cups homemade cashew milk (page 15)

2 tablespoons coconut sugar

⅛ teaspoon vanilla liquid stevia

contents of enough dairy-free probiotic capsules to equal about 37 billion

special equipment: candy thermometer

note

This recipe makes just under 8 cups of Yogurt Drink, which is enough for several batches of frozen yogurt. I like to make a lot so we can drink it, too. Cut the recipe in half if you prefer to make less.

1 Add the coconut milk, cashew milk, coconut sugar, and liquid stevia to a large saucepan. Bring to a simmer over medium heat, watching carefully so that it doesn't boil over.

2 Simmer for 1 minute, then turn off the heat and let the mixture cool.

3 Use a candy thermometer to monitor the temperature. When the thermometer reads 92°F, whisk in the contents of the probiotic capsules.

4 Transfer the mixture to a large glass container with a lid. Set it aside.

5 Sandwich a heating pad between 2 kitchen towels on the counter, and place the glass container on top.

6 Plug in the heating pad and set it on low to medium-low heat. It should make the bottom of the container warm, but not hot.

7 The Yogurt Drink will be ready to refrigerate in 12 to 24 hours, or when its taste is to your liking. (It will become more sour as it sits.)

tip

I've tried this recipe with other milk substitutes and did not have good results. Cashew and coconut milk work wonderfully.

Apricot Amaretto Frozen Yogurt

I love amaretto extract. It takes this apricot yogurt flavor to a whole new level.

6 ounces organic dried apricots

1 cup water, plus more as needed

¼ cup (about 4) soft, pitted Medjool dates

2 cups Yummy Yogurt Drink (page 134) or store-bought dairy-free yogurt

1 teaspoon lemon juice

¼ teaspoon amaretto extract

MAKES 1 TO 1½ QUARTS

1 Soak the apricots in 1 cup water for about 8 hours.

2 Put the apricots and their soaking water, dates, Yogurt Drink or yogurt, lemon juice, and amaretto extract in a blender or food processor. Add more water as needed until you reach the 4-cup line on the blender or food processor. Purée until smooth.

3 Freeze for no more than 30 minutes.

4 Pour into the ice cream machine and churn per the manufacturer's instructions.

5 Eat right away or freeze until hard for pretty scoops.

Lemon-Lime Frozen Yogurt

This citrusy frozen yogurt is so refreshing on a really hot summer day.

1¼ cups coconut water (see Tip)

½ cup (about 8) soft, pitted Medjool dates

2 cups Yummy Yogurt Drink (page 134) or store-bought dairy-free yogurt

1 tablespoon lemon juice

1 tablespoon lime juice

1 teaspoon vanilla extract

½ to 1 teaspoon finely grated lemon or lime zest, as desired

little pinch of fine-grain sea salt

optional: thickener (page 19)

MAKES 1 TO 1½ QUARTS

1 Put the coconut water and dates in a blender and purée until smooth.

2 Add the Yogurt Drink or yogurt, lemon juice, lime juice, vanilla extract, lemon or lime zest, salt, and thickener (if using). Purée until smooth.

3 Freeze for about an hour or refrigerate until cold.

4 Pour into the ice cream machine and churn per the manufacturer's instructions.

5 Eat right away or freeze until hard for pretty scoops.

tip **Directions for getting fresh coconut water can be found on page 194.**

Orange Cream Frozen Yogurt

Orange Cream or Orange Julius is delicious already, but I make mine with Yummy Yogurt Drink, so it's even better.

3 oranges, peeled, segmented, and seeded (about 2 cups)

¼ cup (about 4) soft, pitted Medjool dates

2 cups Yummy Yogurt Drink (page 134) or store-bought dairy-free yogurt

1 teaspoon vanilla extract

MAKES 1 TO 1½ QUARTS

1   Put the oranges and dates in a blender and purée until smooth.

2   Add the Yogurt Drink or yogurt and vanilla extract and purée until smooth.

3   Freeze for about an hour or refrigerate until cold.

4   Pour into the ice cream machine and churn per the manufacturer's instructions.

5   Eat right away or freeze until hard for pretty scoops.

Peach Frozen Yogurt

Fresh peaches give this frozen yogurt an amazing flavor, but frozen peaches are great, too.

4 cups sliced fresh peaches or 20 ounces frozen sliced peaches

2 cups Yummy Yogurt Drink (page 134), plus more as needed

½ cup (about 8) soft, pitted Medjool dates

1 teaspoon lemon juice

1 teaspoon vanilla extract

MAKES 1 TO 1½ QUARTS

1 Put the peaches and Yogurt Drink or yogurt in a blender and purée until smooth.

2 Add the dates, lemon juice, and vanilla extract. Add more Yogurt Drink or yogurt as needed until you reach the 4-cup line on the blender. Purée until smooth.

3 Freeze for about an hour or refrigerate until cold.

4 Pour into the ice cream machine and churn per the manufacturer's instructions.

5 Eat right away or freeze until hard for pretty scoops.

Almond and Chocolate Protein Pudding Pops

To my daughters, Zoe and Ashley, these pudding pops are tied with Grape Sorbet (page 162) for their favorite recipe in this book. Made with almond butter, protein powder, raw cacao powder, and chia seeds, they are incredibly nutrient-dense and often eaten for breakfast at our house.

1½ cups water

¾ cup almond butter (I prefer raw, but roasted also works)

3 soft, pitted Medjool dates

2 tablespoons sweetened protein powder

2 tablespoons organic black cocoa powder

2 tablespoons chia seeds, ground

big pinch of sea salt

special equipment: ice pop molds—set of 6 (page 23)

MAKES 6 POPS

1   Place all the ingredients in a blender or food processor and purée until smooth.

2   Pour into the molds, add the sticks, and freeze.

3   To remove the pops from the molds, place them in a bowl of very hot water for 10 seconds or more to loosen them.

We have used Vitol Egg Protein Powder for many years, and it's still our favorite. However, any protein powder will work. If you're using a professional blender, like a Blendtec or Vitamix, you can add your chia seeds without grinding them first. If you use unsweetened protein powder, omit the chia seeds and double the dates.

Don't force a pop out of the mold if it isn't ready, or you may end up removing only the stick.

Refresh the hot soaking water (used to remove the pops from the molds) as needed to maintain lots of heat. This way, the surface of the pops melt quickly so they can be removed, but the middle stays frozen.

Cherry Yogurt Ice Pops

The truth is that I made these pops because I thought they would be pretty, and we do eat with our eyes first. They're great for a summer party, and they taste good, too.

1½ cups cherries, fresh or frozen and thawed

2 tablespoons raw honey or raw agave

about 1½ cups Yummy Yogurt Drink (page 134) or store-bought dairy-free yogurt

special equipment: ice pop molds—set of 6 (page 23)

MAKES 6 POPS

1 Place the cherries and honey or agave in a food processor. Pulse to form a chunky spread.

2 Add a couple tablespoons of Yogurt Drink or yogurt to each pop mold, then add a couple tablespoons of the cherry spread.

3 Continue layering until the 6 molds are full. Add the sticks, then freeze.

4 To remove the pops from the molds, place them in a bowl of very hot water for 10 seconds or more to loosen them.

Chocolate Chip Banana Bread Pudding Pops

You know how we make brownies and brownie batter with almond butter? Well, that same ingredient gives these pops a hint of banana bread flavor.

2 tablespoons buttery spread (page 19)

4 small bananas

1 tablespoon lemon juice

1 cup canned full-fat coconut milk

½ cup water

¼ cup almond butter (I prefer raw, but roasted also works)

2 tablespoons raw honey or raw agave

⅛ teaspoon fine-grain sea salt

¼ cup dairy-free dark chocolate chips

special equipment: ice pop molds—set of 6 (page 23)

MAKES 6 POPS

1　Heat a 12-inch frying pan over medium heat, then add the buttery spread.

2　Slice the bananas into ½-inch pieces and lay them flat side down in the pan. Do not disturb them for 3 minutes.

3　Flip the bananas to the other side, and do not disturb them for another 3 minutes.

4　Put the browned bananas, lemon juice, coconut milk, water, almond butter, honey or agave, and salt in a blender. Purée until smooth.

5　When the mixture has cooled, stir in the chocolate chips, then divide it evenly among the 6 pop molds.

6　Add the sticks, then freeze.

7　To remove the pops from the molds, place them in a bowl of very hot water for 10 seconds or more to loosen them.

tip **Sunflower seed butter is also great in these pops—it gives them a peanut butter and banana kind of flavor.**

Chocolate-Covered Kiwi and Banana Pops

These pops are really fun and easy enough for kids to make on their own, especially since even a butter knife can cut these fruits.

3 kiwi fruits

1 banana

1 batch Chocolate Crackle (page 172)

special equipment: ice pop molds—set of 6 (page 23)

MAKES 4 POPS

1 Cut each kiwi in half. Run a spoon around the edge where the skin meets the fruit to scoop out each half in one piece.

2 Slice the bananas into about 1-inch pieces.

3 Insert a lollipop stick lengthwise into a slice of banana, and then lengthwise into one of the kiwi halves, and then lengthwise into another banana. Repeat this order on a second stick.

4 Insert a lollipop stick lengthwise into a kiwi half, then lengthwise into a slice of banana, and then lengthwise into another kiwi half. Repeat this order on a second stick.

5 Lay the fruit sticks on their sides on a baking sheet lined with unbleached parchment paper. Freeze until hard.

6 Drizzle the Chocolate Crackle over the frozen fruit sticks, then return them to the freezer to harden for several minutes.

7 When the chocolate is firm, turn the sticks over and drizzle chocolate on the other side as well.

8 Eat right away or store in the freezer. Let frozen fruit pops thaw for about 10 minutes before eating.

Kiwi Apricot Mango Pops

Fresh fruit pops are so easy, healthy, and pretty. Simply purée fresh fruit, layer, and freeze.

1 cup each kiwi, apricot, and mango puree, or 3 cups puréed fruit of your choice

special equipment: ice pop molds—set of 6 (page 23)

MAKES 6 POPS

1 Divide the kiwi puree evenly among 6 ice pop molds.

2 Divide the apricot puree and then the mango puree evenly among the molds.

3 Add the sticks, then freeze.

4 To remove the pops from the molds, place them in a bowl of very hot water for 10 seconds or more to loosen them.

tip **When you're making pops for a party, I recommend removing them from their molds ahead of time. After you remove the pops from the molds, put each pop in a sandwich-sized wax paper bag, then put them back in the freezer until it's time to serve them.**

Rainbow Pops

My eleven-year-old squeals with excitement at the mere sight of these Rainbow Pops. I have to admit, I'm thirty-six and I get pretty excited about them, too.

FOR THE MAGENTA LAYER
1 cup packed sliced fresh strawberries

2 soft, pitted Medjool dates

1 teaspoon lemon juice

2 tablespoons canned full-fat coconut milk

optional: 1 tablespoon cranberry powder (for a boost of color)

FOR THE ORANGE LAYER
3 tablespoons goji berries, soaked in water for 20 minutes and then strained

2 soft, pitted Medjool dates

½ cup water

2 tablespoons canned full-fat coconut milk

FOR THE YELLOW LAYER
1 tablespoon Orange Layer (above)

2 soft, pitted Medjool dates

½ cup water

2 tablespoons canned full-fat coconut milk

FOR THE GREEN LAYER
2 tablespoons packed fresh mint leaves

¼ cup water, just off the boil

7 kiwi fruits

1 teaspoon lemon juice

1 soft, pitted Medjool date

FOR THE PURPLE LAYER
¼ cup raisins, preferably black raisins (see Tip)

¼ cup water

¼ cup fresh blueberries

2 soft, pitted Medjool dates

¼ cup canned full-fat coconut milk

1 tablespoon lemon juice

special equipment: ice pop molds—set of 6 (page 23)

MAKES ABOUT 8 POPS

tip

As long as you make the colors in this order, you don't need to clean the food processor before making the next layer.

Adding lemon juice to the Magenta, Green, and Purple layers helps the fruits retain their color.

I think that black raisins (like Black Beauty raisins) create a color that is more complementary to the other layers; however, you can substitute a cup of fresh blueberries if you prefer a lighter purple.

MAKE THE LAYERS

1   Put the ingredients for the Magenta Layer in a food processor fitted with an S-shaped blade.

2   Purée until smooth, then use a flexible silicone spatula to transfer the puree to a small bowl.

3   Put the ingredients for the Orange Layer in the food processor.

4   Purée until smooth, then use a flexible silicone spatula to transfer the puree to another small bowl.

5   Put the ingredients for the Yellow Layer in the food processor.

6   Purée until smooth, then use a flexible silicone spatula to transfer the puree to another small bowl.

7   To make the Green Layer, put the mint leaves in a small bowl and cover them with the hot water. Cover the bowl and let sit for 10 minutes. (Soaking the mint leaves in hot water allows them to be completely puréed. Skipping this step will result in green flecks and a less vibrant shade of green.)

8   Strain the mint leaves and put them in the food processor.

9   Cut each kiwi in half lengthwise (from end to end). Use a paring knife to carve out the middle, including the seeds, so that it looks like a canoe. Use a spoon to scrape any seeds that are left behind and discard them. (Scraping the seeds from end to end is more effective than scraping them from one side to the other.)

10 Using the spoon, scoop out the kiwi and add it to the food processor with the mint leaves.

11 Add the lemon juice and date and purée until smooth. Use a flexible silicone spatula to transfer the puree to another small bowl.

12 Put the raisins and water in a small saucepan and simmer over low to medium heat for 5 minutes.

13 Put the raisins and water in the food processor. Add the blueberries, dates, coconut milk, and lemon juice. Purée until smooth.

14 Use a flexible silicone spatula to transfer the puree to another small bowl.

CREATE THE POPS

1   Add a couple spoonfuls of the Magenta Layer to each pop mold, then freeze the pops for 30 minutes.

2   Add a couple spoonfuls of the Orange Layer to each pop mold, then freeze the pops for 30 minutes.

3   Continue layering the colors and freezing for 30 minutes between layers. After you add the Green Layer, insert a wooden Popsicle stick into each pop. Press the sticks down slightly into the frozen Yellow Layer to help them stand up.

4   After you add the Purple Layer to the frozen Green Layer, freeze the pops overnight.

5   To remove the pops from the molds, place them in a bowl of very hot water for 10 seconds or more to loosen them.

Watermelon Fruit Pops

These pretty fruit pops are naturally red from the watermelon purée.

about 2 cups cubed seedless watermelon (or watermelon with seeds removed)

3 kiwi fruits

½ cup blueberries, fresh or frozen and thawed

1 banana, sliced into pieces just wide enough to fit in the mold

MAKES 6 POPS

1 Put the watermelon in a blender and purée until smooth. Set aside.

2 Cut each kiwi in half. Run a spoon around the edge where the skin meets the fruit to scoop out each half in one piece. Cut each half in half again lengthwise if the kiwi won't fit in the pop mold.

3 Divide the kiwi pieces, banana slices, and blueberries among the 6 molds. To ensure that the kiwi and banana are the most visible after freezing, press them against the sides of the molds.

4 Fill the molds with watermelon purée, add the sticks, then freeze.

5 To remove the pops from the molds, place them in a bowl of very hot water for 10 seconds or more to loosen them.

Coconut Water Sherbet

Fresh or raw coconut water is indescribably delicious, but packaged coconut water can also be very good if you try not to compare the two.

2½ cups coconut water (see Tip)

½ cup (about 8) soft, pitted Medjool dates

1 cup canned full-fat coconut milk

2 teaspoons lemon or lime juice

optional: thickener (page 19)

MAKES 1 TO 1½ QUARTS

1 Put the coconut water and dates in a blender and purée until smooth.

2 Add the coconut milk, lemon or lime juice, and thickener (if using). Purée until smooth.

3 Freeze for about an hour or refrigerate until cold.

4 Pour into the ice cream machine and churn per the manufacturer's instructions.

5 Eat right away or freeze until hard for pretty scoops.

tip **Directions for getting fresh coconut water can be found on page 194.**

Grape Sorbet

The combination of 100-percent juice and dates makes this sorbet and the Pomegranate Sorbet on page 166 two of the sweetest recipes in this book. And if you remember from the introduction, the more sugar it contains, the softer your frozen treat will be. These sorbets need no time to thaw. You can take them out of the freezer and scoop right away.

3 cups organic 100-percent Concord grape juice, divided

½ cup (about 8) soft, pitted Medjool dates

1 teaspoon lemon juice

optional: thickener (page 19)

MAKES 1 TO 1½ QUARTS

1 Put half the grape juice and all the dates in a blender and purée until smooth.

2 Add the other half of the grape juice and the lemon juice. Purée until smooth.

3 Freeze for about an hour or refrigerate until cold.

4 Pour into the ice cream machine and churn per the manufacturer's instructions.

5 Eat right away or freeze until hard for pretty scoops.

Persimmon Sherbet

If you love persimmons as much as I do, then I know you will appreciate this Persimmon Sherbet.

───────────────────────────

1 (13.5-ounce) can full-fat coconut milk

½ cup (about 8) soft, pitted Medjool dates

1½ cups Persimmon Compote (page 182)

1½ teaspoons lemon juice

FOR SERVING (OPTIONAL)
additional Persimmon Compote

Toasted Coconut Flakes (page 200)

MAKES 1 TO 1½ QUARTS

1 Add the coconut milk and dates to a blender and purée until smooth.

2 Add the Persimmon Compote and lemon juice to the blender. Purée until smooth.

3 Freeze for no more than 30 minutes.

4 Pour into the ice cream machine and churn per the manufacturer's instructions.

5 Eat right away or freeze until hard for pretty scoops. Top the sherbet with more Persimmon Compote and Toasted Coconut Flakes, if you wish.

Pomegranate Sorbet

You can use any flavor of 100-percent juice when making sorbet, but pomegranate and grape juice are our favorites.

3 cups organic 100-percent pomegranate juice, divided (see Tip)

½ cup (about 8) soft, pitted Medjool dates

1 teaspoon lemon juice

optional: thickener (page 19)

MAKES 1 TO 1½ QUARTS

1 Put half the pomegranate juice and all the dates in a blender and purée until smooth.

2 Add the other half of the pomegranate juice and the lemon juice. Purée until smooth.

3 Freeze for about an hour or refrigerate until cold.

4 Pour into the ice cream machine and churn per the manufacturer's instructions.

5 Eat right away or freeze until hard for pretty scoops.

tip **I prefer the R. W. Knudsen brand of pomegranate juice.**

Strawberry Rhubarb Sherbet

The idea to make Strawberry Rhubarb Sherbet came to me one day when I was testing recipes for this book. I reached into the freezer to grab a bag of frozen strawberries and saw frozen rhubarb. If you love strawberry rhubarb pie as much as I do, then you'll love this sherbet, too.

3 cups (10 ounces) frozen sliced rhubarb

2 cups (10 ounces) frozen whole strawberries

2 teaspoons lemon juice

⅛ teaspoon fine-grain sea salt

½ cup (about 8) soft, pitted Medjool dates

1 cup almond, cashew, or hemp milk

½ cup canned full-fat coconut milk

1 teaspoon vanilla extract

1 teaspoon ground cinnamon

MAKES 1 TO 1½ QUARTS

1   In a medium-sized saucepan set over medium-low heat, combine the rhubarb, strawberries, lemon juice, and salt.

2   Cover and cook for about 10 minutes, stirring occasionally.

3   Put the cooked fruit, plus all the liquid in the pan, in a blender and purée until smooth.

4   Add the dates, almond, cashew, or hemp milk, coconut milk, vanilla extract, and cinnamon to the blender. Purée until smooth.

5   Freeze for about an hour or refrigerate until cold.

6   Pour into the ice cream machine and churn per the manufacturer's instructions.

7   Eat right away or freeze until hard for pretty scoops.

Sauces & Sprinkled Toppings

Chocolate Crackle

This thin chocolate sauce will harden quickly after you pour it over your ice cream. Then you can crack it with the back of your spoon and eat a piece with every bite of ice cream.

1 ounce dairy-free dark chocolate

1 tablespoon coconut sugar, ground in a spice grinder

2 tablespoons melted coconut oil

MAKES JUST OVER ¼ CUP

1 Melt the chocolate, sugar, and coconut oil over a double boiler.

2 Remove from the heat, stir, and pour over ice cream.

Chocolate Hazelnut Spread

The first time I had Chocolate Hazelnut Spread was when I visited Rome in my early twenties. I ordered it on a fresh hot crepe—a common treat in Italy and other parts of Europe. My eyes bugged out of my head as I devoured the plateful. Many years later, I challenged myself to re-create Chocolate Hazelnut Spread in a healthier version with a third of the sugar and no dairy. I'm sure you will love the result.

1½ cups hazelnuts

1½ (13.5-ounce) cans full-fat coconut milk

½ cup coconut sugar

¼ teaspoon fine-grain sea salt

3 (3-ounce) bars 70-percent dairy-free dark chocolate

MAKES ABOUT 4 CUPS

1 Preheat the oven to 350°F. Spread the hazelnuts on a baking sheet and toast in the oven for about 20 minutes, until the skins are beginning to flake off.

2 While the hazelnuts are toasting, place the coconut milk, coconut sugar, and salt in a small saucepan over medium heat. When the sugar has melted, remove the pan from the heat and set it aside.

3 Over a double boiler, melt the chocolate bars and set them aside.

4 Remove the toasted hazelnuts from the oven and let them cool slightly. Rub the hazelnuts in a clean, dry kitchen towel to remove as much of the skins as possible.

5 Add the hazelnuts to a food processor and purée until very fine.

6 Add the melted chocolate bars to the food processor and purée until smooth (about 2 minutes).

7 Add the milk mixture to the food processor and purée until smooth.

8 Store in mason jars in the refrigerator for up to 2 weeks. This spread also freezes well.

Ganache

Ganache is traditionally made by pouring hot cream over chopped chocolate and whisking to combine them. I make mine the same way, using coconut milk and fairly traded dark chocolate.

⅔ cup canned full-fat coconut milk

3 ounces dairy-free dark chocolate, chopped

MAKES ABOUT 1 CUP

1   In a small saucepan over medium heat, warm the coconut milk until it begins to simmer.

2   Place the chocolate in a bowl, pour the hot coconut milk over it, and let it sit for 1 to 2 minutes.

3   Whisk as the heat of the coconut milk melts the chocolate. Continue whisking until the milk and chocolate are well combined.

4   Store covered at room temperature for up to 1 week.

 Do not attempt to make Ganache with almond milk or lite coconut milk; it will not work.

Honey Marshmallow Fluff

This Honey Marshmallow Fluff is for those of you who eat Paleo, like I do. For vegan fluff, I recommend Suzanne's Ricemellow Creme. This recipe is based on my friend Jenni's Honey Marshmallows. You can find all of Jenni's amazing recipes on TheUrbanPoser.com.

1 cup water, divided

1 tablespoon gelatin

1 teaspoon vanilla extract

¼ teaspoon fine-grain sea salt

1 cup raw honey

special equipment: candy thermometer

MAKES ABOUT 2 CUPS

1 In a large, deep mixing bowl, combine ½ cup of the water with the gelatin, vanilla extract, and salt. Set aside.

2 In a small, heavy-bottomed saucepan, bring the remaining ½ cup water and the honey to a simmer.

3 Use a candy thermometer to monitor the temperature of the honey mixture. When the thermometer reads 240°F, put on a pair of oven mitts and very carefully pour the honey mixture into the mixing bowl with the other ingredients.

4 Still wearing the oven mitts, beat with a handheld electric mixer (a stand mixer also works) until it is fluffy and almost doubled in size, about 8 minutes.

5 Store covered at room temperature for up to several days.

Warmed Nut or Seed Butter Sauce

When thinned with water to sauce consistency, nut and seed butters make yummy toppings for ice cream. You can even add cocoa powder and honey or agave.

¼ cup almond butter or sunflower seed butter, without added sugar

¼ cup water, plus more as needed

big pinch of fine-grain sea salt

MAKES ABOUT ¾ CUP

1 Add the almond butter or sunflower seed butter to a small saucepan. Turn the heat to medium and slowly add the water.

2 Stir and continue to heat, adding more water until the sauce reaches the desired consistency.

3 Remove from the heat and stir in the salt.

4 Store leftover sauce in the refrigerator for up to about 2 weeks..

tip **Nut and seed butters should always be stored in the refrigerator to keep their oils from turning rancid.**

Persimmon Compote

I ate my first persimmon when we moved to Colorado. Here in California, persimmons are everywhere, and I couldn't be happier about that. You can find persimmons at grocery stores and farmers' markets in the winter, when they are in season.

6 to 7 ripe Fuyu persimmons (see Tip)

1 tablespoon lemon juice

1 tablespoon maple syrup

little pinch of fine-grain sea salt

MAKES 3 CUPS

1 Remove the persimmon leaves and cut the persimmons into quarters. Discard the seeds if you find any.

2 Place the persimmons, lemon juice, maple syrup, and salt in a blender or food processor and purée until smooth.

3 Taste the compote. If the flavor is bland, put the compote in a small saucepan and simmer, covered, over low to medium heat for about 20 minutes, stirring occasionally. This will heighten the flavor.

4 Store in mason jars in the refrigerator for up to 2 weeks. This compote also freezes well.

tip **Fuyu persimmons are tomato-shaped, not cone-shaped. They are best when ripe but can be eaten crunchy as well. Hachiya persimmons (the cone-shaped ones) must be extremely ripe or they taste very unpleasant.**

Salted Caramel Sauce

1 cup canned full-fat coconut milk

1 cup coconut sugar

¼ teaspoon fine-grain sea salt

MAKES ABOUT 1 CUP

1. In a heavy-bottomed pot that is about 7 inches wide by 3 inches deep, whisk together the coconut milk, coconut sugar, and salt.

2. Bring the mixture to a boil over medium heat. Boil for 15 minutes, watching carefully to make sure that it doesn't boil over.

3. Reduce the heat to low and simmer for 5 minutes, watching carefully to make sure that it doesn't burn. If it begins to burn, the edges will turn dry and black, and you will probably have to throw it out and start over.

4. Wear gloves to pour the hot caramel into a small heat-proof bowl, and stir periodically as it cools to room temperature. Don't wash the pot just yet; you may need it again.

5. If the caramel isn't thick (similar to molasses) when it reaches room temperature (after about 20 minutes), pour it back into the pot and let it simmer over the lowest heat possible for another 3 to 5 minutes.

6. Wear gloves to pour the caramel back into the small bowl, and stir periodically as it cools to room temperature.

7. To reheat leftover caramel (such as for dipping apples or pouring over ice cream), put the bowl of caramel in a larger dish of very hot water, and cover it for 15 minutes. If needed, add more hot water, and repeat.

8. Store covered at room temperature for up to 1 week.

Strawberry Compote

This compote is really easy to make. I've also used other frozen berries with good results.

4 (10-ounce) bags frozen whole strawberries

1 teaspoon lemon juice

¼ cup coconut sugar

1 teaspoon vanilla extract

MAKES 2 CUPS

1   Let the strawberries thaw to room temperature.

2   Place a fine-mesh strainer in a mixing bowl. Add the thawed strawberries to the strainer and press the strawberries down to remove as much liquid as possible.

3   Purée the strawberries slightly, if desired, then add them to a small saucepan along with the lemon juice, coconut sugar, and vanilla extract.

4   Simmer over low to medium heat for 20 minutes, covered, but with the lid cracked 1 inch. Stir about every 5 minutes.

5   Let cool, then store in mason jars in the refrigerator for up to 2 weeks. This compote also freezes well.

tip **If you would rather not make compote, St. Dalfour and Crofter's Just Fruit Spreads are two brands that are free of refined sugar. Heat them in a small saucepan, and thin with water as needed.**

Tart Cranberry Sauce

Have you ever put leftover cranberry sauce over ice cream? I don't mean the canned stuff that looks like a gel blob; I'm talking about the real stuff. Homemade Tart Cranberry Sauce is completely different, and it's really good with ice cream.

16 ounces fresh cranberries

2 tablespoons finely grated orange zest

2 cinnamon sticks

1 cup fresh-squeezed orange juice

½ cup coconut sugar

big pinch of fine-grain sea salt

optional: ¼ teaspoon ground ginger

MAKES JUST OVER 2 CUPS

1 Remove any crushed or bad cranberries, then place the cranberries in a medium-sized heavy-bottomed pot.

2 Add the orange zest, cinnamon sticks, orange juice, coconut sugar, salt, and ginger (if using).

3 Simmer, uncovered, for about 20 minutes.

4 Remove and discard the cinnamon sticks and let the sauce cool.

5 Store in mason jars in the refrigerator for up to 2 weeks. Cranberry sauce also freezes well.

Whipped Coconut Cream

Whipped Coconut Cream can be made ahead of time. I think it's even better the day after it's made.

---

about 2 cups coconut cream, from packaged coconut milk (recipe follows)

2 teaspoons raw honey or raw agave

vanilla liquid stevia, to taste

optional: 1 teaspoon gelatin that has been completely dissolved into 2 tablespoons boiling water

MAKES SLIGHTLY OVER 2 CUPS

1   Put the coconut cream in a mixing bowl along with the honey or agave and liquid stevia. Beat with a handheld electric mixer until combined.

2   At this point, the Whipped Coconut Cream is ready, but it may look lumpy, even when piped. If you eat gelatin, you can smooth out the texture by mixing in the dissolved gelatin.

3   If you are not using the Whipped Coconut Cream right away, refrigerate it. (If it becomes warm, it will melt.)

4   Cut the tip off of one corner of a plastic food storage bag. Insert an open star piping tip into that corner, then add the Whipped Coconut Cream to the bag.

5   Twist the bag and squeeze to pipe the Whipped Coconut Cream onto ice cream.

6   Store leftover Whipped Coconut Cream in the refrigerator for up to 2 weeks.

Coconut Cream (from packaged coconut milk)

There are two ways to get coconut cream: one is to use the cream that has separated from packaged full-fat coconut milk, and the other is to use fresh young coconuts. While the former method is much easier, it's not foolproof, as not every can or carton of coconut milk will separate. It can be very frustrating!

I created this foolproof technique using the Natural Value and Aroy-D brands, with which I've had luck 100 percent of the time. If you have other brands of canned coconut milk that have separated or will separate after being refrigerated for a day, then by all means use them. For the fresh coconut option, turn the page.

2 (13.5-ounce) cans Natural Value full-fat coconut milk or 1 (33-ounce) carton Aroy-D Coconut Cream (actually a thick 100-percent coconut milk)

MAKES ABOUT 2 CUPS

FOR NATURAL VALUE CANS

1　Chill the cans of coconut milk in the refrigerator overnight.

2　Place a thin cloth napkin over a large mixing bowl, and pour the contents of 1 can over the napkin.

3　Lift the napkin and squeeze out some of the water. Don't overdo the squeezing, or your coconut cream will be too dry. Just remove most of the water.

4　Repeat Steps 2 and 3 with the second can of chilled coconut milk. When you open the napkin, your coconut cream should look like a ball of soft cheese.

FOR AROY-D COCONUT CREAM CARTONS

1　Chill the carton in the refrigerator overnight. If the Aroy-D does not separate, pour it into a bowl and freeze it.

2　Thaw the cream on the kitchen counter. Do not heat it, or it will re-emulsify.

3　Place a thin cloth napkin over a large mixing bowl, and pour the cream over the napkin.

4　Lift the napkin and squeeze out some of the water. Don't overdo the squeezing, or your coconut cream will be too dry. Just remove most of the water.

5　When you open the napkin, your coconut cream should look like a ball of soft cheese.

Coconut Cream (from fresh young coconuts)

Fresh puréed coconut tastes far superior to coconut cream from packaged coconut milk in my opinion, but it takes longer to make, it costs more, and the thickness is less consistent since some coconut meat is drier than others.

at least 3 whole fresh young coconuts (the white ones with pointy tops)

MAKES ABOUT 1½ CUPS

note The coconut water should be clear or slightly yellow. Pink or purple water means that the coconut has gone bad, and you shouldn't use the water or the meat.

1 Lay a coconut on its side, and carefully trim the pointy tip until some brown is showing. Then position it right side up.

2 As a safety measure, put your left hand behind your back (or your right hand if you're left-handed). Doing so protects you from the knife.

3 Using the heel of a knife, strike the coconut at a 45-degree angle.

4 If the top doesn't open right away, spin the coconut a little bit, put one hand behind your back, and strike it again. Continue until you are able to pry open the top.

5 Pour the nutritious coconut water into a large glass. I put mine in big mason jars. Store what you don't drink right away in the refrigerator.

6 Wedge a flexible silicone spatula between the meat and the inside wall of the coconut. Run the spatula around in a circle, dislodging the coconut meat.

7 Reach inside the coconut and remove the meat. It usually comes out in one piece.

8 Repeat the process with 2 or more coconuts.

9 In a food processor fitted with an S-shaped blade, purée the coconut meat, scraping the sides periodically, until it is completely smooth and heavenly.

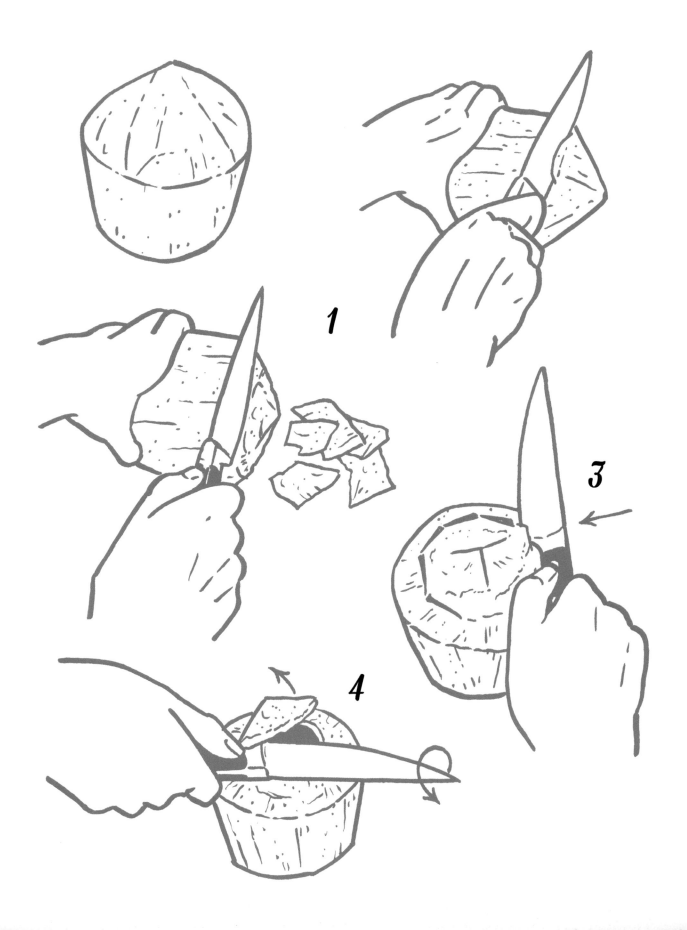

Dairy-Free Dark Chocolate Chips and Shavings

To make chocolate shavings, I use a vegetable peeler to peel shavings off of bars of dark chocolate. My favorite chocolate bars are Alter Eco (85-percent cacao), Equal Exchange (80-percent cacao), and Green & Black (85-percent cacao), all of which were organic, fairly traded, and free of soy lecithin at the time this book was printed. (If you haven't done so already, please check out page 20, where I talk about the importance of ethically sourced chocolate.)

Dagoba is one of the few brands that makes dairy-free chocolate chips with a decent amount of cacao in them. I don't like to go lower than 70 percent, and Dagoba chips are 74-percent cacao. However, more and more brands are recognizing the desire for good dark chocolate chips, so keep a eye out. And you can always chop dairy-free dark chocolate bars into "chips" yourself.

1 Hold your vegetable peeler as you normally would for peeling.

2 In your other hand, hold a bar of dairy-free dark chocolate.

3 Scrape the peeler down the long side of the chocolate bar for small curls and shavings.

 To get larger curls, warm the bar to soften it slightly before peeling. Refrigerate larger curls (from softened chocolate) in order to set.

Freeze-Dried Strawberries

Freeze-dried strawberries are delicious on their own, but with the help of a Magic Bullet blender or coffee grinder, they become pretty rose-colored sprinkles. They look incredible on ice cream, Whipped Coconut Cream (page 190), and piped frosting. Simply grind freeze-dried strawberries in a clean, dry Magic Bullet blender or coffee grinder and sprinkle. So cute!

1 cup freeze-dried strawberries

MAKES ABOUT ¼ CUP POWDER

1 Add the freeze-dried strawberries to a clean, dry Magic Bullet blender or coffee grinder. If you are using a coffee grinder, add the strawberries ½ cup at a time.

2 Grind into a powder to be used as sprinkles.

Toasted Coconut Flakes and Sliced Almonds

Toasting coconut flakes and sliced almonds takes them from pretty good to really great. I don't bother preheating the oven first, but of course you can toast coconut flakes and almonds in an oven that is already hot.

1 Spread either unsweetened coconut flakes or unsweetened sliced almonds in a single layer on a rimmed baking sheet.

2 Place the baking sheet in the oven, then turn the oven to 350°F.

3 Stir every few minutes, keeping a close eye on them to make sure that they don't burn.

4 Coconut flakes toast in about 12 minutes, and sliced almonds toast in about 18 minutes.

Fresh Fruit

Bananas, strawberries, and blueberries are some of my favorite fresh fruit toppings for ice cream. Below I have suggested some of my favorite pairings.

FAVORITE FRESH FRUIT PAIRINGS FOR ICE CREAM

1. Fresh cherries on Bing Cherry Ice Cream (page 32)
2. Fresh blueberries on Blueberry Lavender Ice Cream (page 34)
3. Fresh strawberries and raspberries on Chocolate Ice Cream (page 30)
4. Fresh pineapple on Piña Colada Ice Cream (page 48)
5. Fresh bananas on Fried Banana Ice Cream (page 54)
6. Fresh strawberries, blueberries, and bananas on Strawberry Ice Cream (page 64)
7. Fresh strawberries, blueberries, and bananas on Vanilla Ice Cream (page 28)

FAVORITE FRESH FRUIT PAIRINGS FOR FROZEN YOGURT, SHERBET, AND SORBET

1. Fresh bananas and cherries on Apricot Amaretto Frozen Yogurt (page 136)
2. Fresh peaches on Peach Frozen Yogurt (page 142)
3. Fresh strawberries, blueberries, and bananas on Coconut Water Sherbet (page 160)
4. Fresh strawberries, blueberries, and bananas on Grape Sorbet (page 162)
5. Fresh strawberries, blueberries, and bananas on Pomegranate Sorbet (page 166)
6. Fresh strawberries on Strawberry Rhubarb Sherbet (page 168)

Nuts and Seeds

Pistachios, sunflower seeds, walnuts, pecans, almonds, and hazelnuts add flavor and crunch to ice cream. Raw nuts and seeds are good, but roasted and salted nuts and seeds have more intense flavor.

FAVORITE PAIRINGS:

1 Pecans on Butter Pecan Ice Cream (page 36)

2 Pistachios, sunflower seeds, walnuts, pecans, almonds, and/or hazelnuts on Chocolate Ice Cream (page 30)

3 Hazelnuts on Chocolate Hazelnut Ice Cream (page 38)

4 Pecans on Pecan Praline Ice Cream (page 46)

5 Pistachios on Pistachio Ice Cream (page 50)

6 Pistachios, sunflower seeds, walnuts, pecans, almonds, and/or hazelnuts on Fried Banana Ice Cream (page 54)

7 Pistachios, sunflower seeds, walnuts, pecans, almonds, and/or hazelnuts on Rocky Road Ice Cream (page 56)

8 Sunflower seeds on SunButter Fudge Ripple Ice Cream (page 66)

9 Almonds on Swiss Almond Ice Cream (page 68)

10 Pistachios, sunflower seeds, walnuts, pecans, almonds, and/or hazelnuts on Toasted Coconut Ice Cream (page 70)

11 Pistachios, sunflower seeds, walnuts, pecans, almonds, and/or hazelnuts on Vanilla Ice Cream (page 28)

12 Pistachios, sunflower seeds, walnuts, pecans, almonds, and/or hazelnuts on Brownie Batter Ice Cream (page 100)

13 Walnuts on Carrot Cake Ice Cream (page 102)

Ice cream scoop box from the 1950s.

Acknowledgments

To my publisher and team at Victory Belt: Thank you so much for always believing in me and for making my books so beautiful.

♥

To my editors, Holly and Pam: Your suggestions made an enormous difference in the quality of this book. I am so grateful.

♥

To my mom, my mother-in-law, and my friend Elana: Thank you so much for all the treasures you found, which made the photos so lovely.

♥

To Cheryl, my first nutrition mentor: Thank you for bringing to my attention that eating the wrong foods was hurting us and for teaching me that the right foods could transform our health.

♥

To Dr. Murphy, our dear friend and teacher of courage: Thank you for all your love, support, and guidance. You and Andy are the greatest gifts Tyler gave me.

♥

To George: Thank you for taking such great portraits of me. It meant so much to me.

♥

To my fellow bloggers and authors who have become close personal friends: I appreciate you so much. I don't believe we can do this job on our own. Thank you for making what I do possible.

♥

To my husband, Andrew: I could not have done any of this without you. I love you so much. Thank you for being the best partner I could ever imagine.

♥

To my little girls: If it were not for you, I would never have become such a mad scientist in the kitchen. I learn so much from you every day. I love you.

♥

To Rina: Thank you for lending me your gorgeous kitchen for my portraits and for all your help.

♥

To my readers, who tested and suggested so many of the recipes in this book: Thank you so much for coming on this journey to health with me. Healing my family through food and helping you with similar struggles has been the most rewarding challenge of my life.

♥

Resources

You can find all my tools in one place: www.thespunkycoconut.com/spunky-coconut-kitchen-tools/.

Below are the companies I turn to for ingredients. I usually buy their products from Amazon.com, AzureStandard.com, and iHerb.com.

APRICOTS (dried, organic, unsulfured)
www.madeinnature.com

BUTTERY SPREAD

lactose- and casein-free ghee (not for vegans)
www.purityfarms.com

organic coconut spread and soy-free buttery spread
www.earthbalancenatural.com

CHOCOLATE
(organic and Fair Trade [see page 20])

Alter Eco
www.alterecofoods.com

Equal Exchange
www.equalexchange.coop

Green & Black's
www.greenandblacks.com

COCOA POWDER
(organic and Fair Trade [see page 20])
www.frontiercoop.com

COCONUT FLAKES
www.edwardandsons.com

COCONUT MILK

BPA-free cans
www.naturalvalue.com

BPA-free cartons
Aroy-D Coconut Cream
Local Asian grocery stores

COCONUT SUGAR
www.bigtreefarms.com

COFFEE (organic, decaf, Fair Trade)
www.equalexchange.coop

EXTRACTS

Almond extract
www.frontiercoop.com

Amaretto extract
www.olivenation.com

Mint flavor (with spearmint)
www.frontiercoop.com

Vanilla extract
www.flavorganics.com

DATES (Medjool)
www.medjooldates.com

FIGS (dried, organic, Calimyrna figs)
www.madeinnature.com

FOOD COLORING (natural)
www.indiatree.com

FREEZE-DRIED STRAWBERRIES
www.naturesallfoods.com

GELATIN (dairy-free, but not vegetarian)
www.greatlakesgelatin.com

GOJI BERRIES
www.navitasnaturals.com

GUAR GUM
www.bobsredmill.com

HONEYSUCKLE (*Flos Lonicerae;* dried)
**Search on Amazon.com or try
Asian markets**

LAVENDER (dried, culinary)
www.olivenation.com

LOOSE-LEAF JASMINE TEA
www.davidsonstea.com
**Search on Amazon.com or try
Asian markets**

MULLING SPICES
www.frontiercoop.com

PROBIOTICS (dairy-free)
www.klaire.com

RAISINS (black, organic)
www.rawlife.com

STEVIA (non-GMO, chemical-free)
www.nowfoods.com
www.nunaturals.com
www.sweetleaf.com

Recipe Index

PECAN PRALINE ICE CREAM

PIÑA COLADA ICE CREAM

PISTACHIO ICE CREAM

PUMPKIN ICE CREAM

FRIED BANANA ICE CREAM

ROCKY ROAD ICE CREAM

RUM RAISIN ICE CREAM

**SAFFRON AND ROSE
ICE CREAM**

**SALTED CARAMEL CHOCOLATE
CHUNK ICE CREAM**

STRAWBERRY ICE CREAM

**SUNBUTTER FUDGE
RIPPLE ICE CREAM**

SWISS ALMOND ICE CREAM

TOASTED COCONUT ICE CREAM

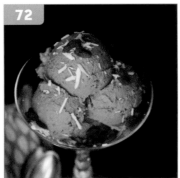

WHITE CHOCOLATE GOJI BERRY ICE CREAM

COFFEE & TEA

COFFEE ICE CREAM & MOCHA ALMOND FUDGE ICE CREAM

CHAI ICE CREAM

EARL GREY TEA ICE CREAM

GINGER KOMBUCHA TEA ICE CREAM

HONEYSUCKLE ICE CREAM

JASMINE TEA ICE CREAM

MATCHA ICE CREAM

ROOIBOS TEA ICE CREAM

MULLED CIDER ICE CREAM

FROZEN COFFEE OR TEA LATTE

CAKES & COOKIES

BROWNIES à la MODE

**BROWNIE BATTER ICE CREAM
& BROWNIE BATTER**

CARROT CAKE ICE CREAM

104

COOKIE BOWLS

106

CHOCOLATE CHIP COOKIES

108

CHOCOLATE CHIP COOKIE DOUGH ICE CREAM

110

CHOCOLATE CHIP ICE CREAM SANDWICHES

112

FROZEN MINT CHOCOLATE WHOOPIE PIES

114

CHOCOLATE WHOOPIE PIE CAKES

116

FRIED BANANA AND CHOCOLATE ICE CREAM CAKE

118

GINGERBREAD COOKIES

120

GINGERBREAD COOKIE DOUGH ICE CREAM

122

GINGERBREAD ICE CREAM SANDWICHES

124

MINI STRAWBERRY ICE CREAM CAKES WITH CHOCOLATE CRACKLE

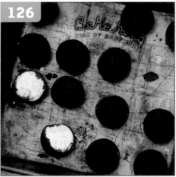
126

MINT WHIPPED CREAM BITES

**N'OATMEAL COOKIE
ICE CREAM SANDWICHES
& N'OATMEAL COOKIES**

**"PEANUT BUTTER" CHOCOLATE
ICE CREAM CAKE**

YOGURT, POPS, & SHERBET

YUMMY YOGURT DRINK

**APRICOT AMARETTO
FROZEN YOGURT**

**LEMON-LIME
FROZEN YOGURT**

**ORANGE CREAM
FROZEN YOGURT**

PEACH FROZEN YOGURT

**ALMOND AND CHOCOLATE
PROTEIN PUDDING POPS**

CHERRY YOGURT ICE POPS

CHOCOLATE CHIP BANANA BREAD PUDDING POPS

CHOCOLATE-COVERED KIWI AND BANANA POPS

KIWI APRICOT MANGO POPS

RAINBOW POPS

WATERMELON FRUIT POPS

COCONUT WATER SHERBET

GRAPE SORBET

PERSIMMON SHERBET

POMEGRANATE SORBET

STRAWBERRY RHUBARB SHERBET

SAUCES & SPRINKLED TOPPINGS

172

CHOCOLATE CRACKLE

174

CHOCOLATE HAZELNUT SPREAD

176

GANACHE

178

HONEY MARSHMALLOW FLUFF

180

**WARMED NUT OR
SEED BUTTER SAUCE**

182

PERSIMMON COMPOTE

184

SALTED CARAMEL SAUCE

186

STRAWBERRY COMPOTE

188

TART CRANBERRY SAUCE

WHIPPED COCONUT CREAM

COCONUT CREAM (FROM PACKAGED COCONUT MILK)

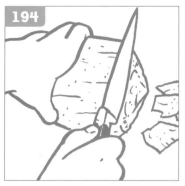

COCONUT CREAM (FROM FRESH YOUNG COCONUTS)

DAIRY-FREE DARK CHOCOLATE CHIPS AND SHAVINGS

FREEZE-DRIED STRAWBERRIES

TOASTED COCONUT FLAKES AND SLICED ALMONDS

FRESH FRUIT

NUTS AND SEEDS

Index